Landscapes of South Africa

THE CAPE

a countryside guide

Peter Rex

SUNFLOWER BOOKS

First published 1998
by Sunflower Books™
12 Kendrick Mews
London SW7 3HG, UK

ISBN 1-85691-117-9

Little Lion's Head (Car tour 2)

Important note to the reader

We have tried to ensure that the descriptions and maps in this book are error-free at press date. The book will be updated, where necessary, whenever future printings permit. It will be very helpful for us to receive your comments (sent in care of the publishers, please) for the updating of future printings.

We also rely on those who use this book — especially walkers — to take along a good supply of common sense when they explore. Conditions change fairly rapidly in the Cape, and ***storm damage or tree felling may make a route unsafe at any time***. If the route is not as described in the book, and your way ahead is not secure, return to the point of departure. ***Never attempt to complete a tour or walk under hazardous conditions!*** Please read carefully the notes on pages 31 to 34, as well as the introductory comments at the beginning of each tour and walk (regarding road conditions, equipment, grade, distances and time, etc). Explore ***safely***, while at the same time respecting the beauty of the countryside.

Cover photograph: the Cape Peninsula coastline, with Lion's Head in the distance
Title page: Protea cynaroides *(king protea)*
Photographs pages 2, 4, 10, 16-17, 18, 20, 23, 27, 67, 74, 88, 101 (top), 111 (bottom): Alchemy; all other photographs: the author
Maps: John Underwood (base information obtained from official maps produced by the Chief Directorate of Surveys and Mapping, South Africa. Reproduced under South African Government Printer's Copyright Authority 10483 dated 8 December 1997.)
A CIP catalogue record for this book is available from the British Library
Printed and bound in the UK by Brightsea Press, Exeter

10 9 8 7 6 5 4 3 2 1

Contents ___

4   Landscapes of the Cape

RECOMMENDED BACKGROUND READING/FIELD GUIDES

Approved paths on Table Mountain (map published by The Mountain Club of South Africa, 1993)

Bickford-Smith *et al: Cape Town: an illustrated social history* (David Philip, 1998)

Burman, L and Bean, A: *Hottentots-Holland to Hermanus — flower guide no 5* (Botanical Society of South Africa, 1985)

Cameron, T and Spies, S B (editors): *A new illustrated history of South Africa* (Southern Book Publishers, 1991)

Kidd, M M: *Cape Peninsula — flower guide no 3* (Botanical Society of South Africa, 1995)

Newman, K: *Birds of southern Africa* (Southern Book Publishers, 1997)

Platter, J and E: *South African wine guide* (Platter, published annually)

Portfolio Collection: *Bed and breakfast, Country places, Retreats* (three booklets available from South African tourist offices)

Street guide: Cape Town (Map Studio, published annually).

View to Table Mountain from the north (Car tour 3)

❋ Preface

The Cape is a term that has almost as many meanings as there are people living in it, for it exists in a social maelstrom, the old certainties swept aside by the new. But in reality it is more than that: its identity has been shaped by geology and climate as much as by human history — forces that have persisted through aeons of time as well as centuries of political and social change. For all practical purposes, the Cape has always been there.

HISTORY

The rocky peninsula at the eye of the Cape was originally known to the outside world as the Cape of Good Hope or the Cape of Storms — so christened by Portuguese sailors groping their way down the west coast of Africa more than 500 years ago. Its stormy coastline was a fearful hazard to the fragile sailing ships that rounded the point at the end of the 15th century — and for hundreds of years afterwards. From time to time those hardy mariners would land and replenish supplies before sailing on, leaving the local Khoikhoi (formerly known as Hottentots) and Bushmen to pursue the nomadic way of life they'd followed for thousands of years before.

It was the Dutch who changed all that — in 1652, when the Dutch East India Company set up a victualling station on the shores of Table Bay. It was a natural harbour then, providing shelter from the high seas of the southern Atlantic. Over time, increasing numbers of settlers arrived from all over Europe, exploring further inland and bartering their way into more and more land and cattle, gradually reducing the influence of the Khoikhoi cattle farmers until they were no more than tenants in their own back garden, in thrall to the company. The Cape Colony was born.

Births are often overshadowed by deaths, and this one was no exception, for all its drama and high promise. It signalled the start of a slow process of extinction for the Khoikhoi. During the next hundred years or so, diseases brought by the settlers radically reduced their numbers; interbreeding with the settlers and imported slaves did the rest. The Bushmen, the archetypal hunters and gatherers, were gradually squeezed out by increased cultivation, forcing them to migrate to sparser terrain to the north.

But these aboriginal people have not been forgotten. The Bushmen have left their stories and paintings, and the Khoikhoi their spiritual and material heirs — the 'Cape Coloureds'. The latter, along with the Malays whose forebears were shipped from Indonesia in the 17th and 18th centuries, have been and still are a vital part of the cultural and commercial tapestry of the Cape.

Meanwhile, the Dutch East India Company's influence was waning by the end of the 18th century. The British, who were anxious to protect their trading routes against the French, took over the colony for the first time in 1795. This event led inevitably to more and more exploration, annexation and development — not only in the Cape, but far beyond. Finally, in 1910, by the Act of Union, those far-flung territories — Cape Province, Natal, Transvaal and the Orange Free State — became the dominion of South Africa, the precursor of today's 'rainbow nation', a colourful gathering of clans from all points of the compass.

Throughout these often turbulent times the Cape has kept its name, which for the purposes of this book describes an irregular quadrant of largely mountainous land radiating 160km/100mi or so from Cape Town to the north and east — roughly corresponding with the territory administered by the Dutch East India Company early in the 18th century. The territory's heart-beat is Cape Town, a sprawling and restless city sitting astride the corridor of low-lying land between the Atlantic and False Bay, at the northern extremity of the peninsula. Towering above the city is Table Mountain, the northernmost point of the Cape of Storms, a feature more than any other that gives the region its sense of identity. A massive granite and sandstone citadel some 280 million years old, the mountain is a veritable paradise for walker and climber alike, with more than 500 different routes to its wide and rambling summit.

CLIMATE, VEGETATION AND GEOLOGY

The Cape is distinct from the rest of the country in many respects, not least in climate and vegetation. For a start, the rain falls during autumn, winter and spring (mid-April to late October), blown in by 'cold fronts' from the northwest, whereas (with the exception of the land bordering the southern shores of the Atlantic and Indian oceans) the rest of the country has its rain in summer. These winter rains, and the long hot summers that follow them, help to produce a flora that is unique: one of the world's six disparate floral kingdoms. This one stretches well beyond the eastern boundary of 'Cape' territory — to a point some 800km/ 500mi to the east, sticking closely to a narrow strip of land between the coast and the dry mountain slopes facing the Little Karoo to the north.

Despite the fact that this kingdom is only a small fraction of one percent of the earth's surface, it comprises one of the most diverse and rich wild gardens in the world. The low-growing bushes are interspersed with reeds and flowers — mostly ericas, *Restionaceae,* proteas and legumes, together with a host of wild flowers, including hundreds of species of geraniums, irises, lilies, daisies and oxalis.

Paradoxically, the *fynbos* (pronounced fainboss), as this rich carpet of plants is called, thrives on thin and acid soils, broken down over time from the underlying rock. The name describes the narrow-leafed plants that retain their moisture by reducing evaporation in a summer heat intense enough to wilt the fields and pastures stitched into the natural wilderness. The bedrock that feeds this wild garden is largely Table Mountain sandstone, overlying deep layers of solid granite. Thin beds of shale and pebbles intersperse too, on top of the granite as well as higher up in the sandstone — relics from an earlier life under the sea. Occasionally, the underlying granite protrudes through the sandstone and shapes the mountainous terrain.

A major feature of the sandstone forming the higher peaks further inland is its folded strata, often exposed to the naked eye — arched like the vaults of a massive cathedral. Here and there, wherever a recent rockfall has occurred, the fresh rock laid bare by the avalanche is tinged a light yellow or red — vivid witness to the piles of rock debris and twisted trees spread-eagled below. These majestic out-crops provide imposing foils to the green carpet of *fynbos* clinging to their feet, as well as the dark evergreen trees growing along the banks of the streams and rivers, drawing their nourishment from the rains blowing in from the sea and the mists from the mountains.

ACKNOWLEDGEMENTS

Obviously the author did not write this book alone: others must carry their share of the blame as well. Chief among them are: Peter Ross, Elsie Esterhuysen, Rodney Davenport and Hannie Van Wieringen, who provided a great deal of material on both the Cape's history and its flora; Walter Powrie, whose hints on mapwork cut several tedious corners (and John Underwood whose expertise cut many more); William, my younger son, whose know-how in the computer field will be sorely missed once he's gone to America; Pat Underwood, my publisher; and lastly, a host of friends and acquaintances who were cajoled into joining the walking, eating and drinking. My heartfelt thanks go to them all.

Picnicking

These picnic suggestions are intended *for motorists* and are linked to the car tours (those on the same stretch of road are labelled a, b, etc). All of these picnic places are highlighted on the touring map with the symbol *P*. If the area is also shown on one of the large-scale *walking* maps, I refer to the appropriate page; the same symbol pinpoints the location.

1 Grove near the Rhodes Memorial (map page 93)
🚗 Follow Car tour 2 (page 15) and turn off to the Rhodes Memorial. Then follow Walk 15 (page 91) to the first jeep track. Turn left along the track for a few hundred metres/yards, to a pretty chestnut grove. *15min on foot.*

2 Kirstenbosch (map reverse of touring map, photos pages 12, 41, 48-9)
🚗 Follow Car tour 1 (page 11) to the gardens. Choose your own picnic spot, and please remove all your litter. *As long or short a stroll as you wish.*

3 Bel Ombre (map page 104, photograph page 102)
🚗 Follow Car tour 1 (page 11) past the top gate to Kirstenbosch. Then take the second turning to the left (Monterey Drive). Take the second left again (Bel Ombre Drive) and park at the side of the road, just after the first left-hand bend. Then follow the path leading right, into a meadow shaded by trees (see Walk 18, page 104, at the 1h25min-point). *2min on foot.*

4a Cape of Good Hope Nature Reserve (touring map)
🚗 Follow Car tour 1 (pages 11-13) to the reserve gates. About 3.3km beyond the gates, there is a signposted picnic area/bench on the right, on a small hillock. *No walking,* but a short circular walk starts nearby.

4b Cape Point (map page 87)
🚗 Follow Car tour 1 (pages 11-13) all the way to the car park at Cape Point and climb the path towards the point. Any number of picnic spots (and some benches) are clustered on the side of the hill. *About 10min on foot.*

5a Oppelskop on Devil's Peak (map page 93, photograph page 97)
🚗 Follow Car tour 2 (pages 15-16) to Kloofnek, the saddle between Lion's Head and Table Mountain. Then turn left and drive along Tafelbergweg, which runs past the cable station. Turn the car round when the tar ends and park in the third lay-by on the right on the way back (only a few hundred metres from the turning point). The path up to Oppelskop, a rocky buttress, lies on the other side of the road, about 100m/yds back uphill. It joins the lower traverse path a few metres above the road and then zigzags up to the right. After 20min leave the traverse and take a path to the left, which continues rising until it reaches Oppelskop Ridge. Take a short path down to a stone ruin on the top of the rock, from where there is an outstanding view. *35min of steady climbing on foot.*

5b The cannons on Tafelbergweg (map page 93) 🚗
🚗 as for (5a) above. The picnic spot is by a couple of old cannons below the road, almost opposite the path to Oppelskop. *4min on foot.*

5c Signal Hill (map page 99, photographs page 101) 🚗
🚗 Follow (5a) above, but turn right to Signal Hill. *No walking.*

6a Chapman's Peak Drive (map page 65, photograph page 18) 🚗
🚗 There are several good picnic spots on the way to the summit of the

drive after leaving Hout Bay (see Car tour 2, pages 16-17) — including a particularly scenic one at the summit itself, on the right. *No walking.*

6b Ou Kaapseweg (map pages 76-77, photograph below)

🚌 There is a fine picnic spot at the summit of the pass, on the left-hand side of the road (signposted). See Car tours 1 and 2. *No walking.* See also page 82 for more nearby picnic areas, near the start of Walk 12.

7a Bain's Kloof Pass — western slopes (touring map) 🚌

🚌 Follow Car tour 4 (pages 21-22) to Bain's Kloof Pass. There are picnic spots galore on the way up (beyond Wellington). *No walking.*

7b Bain's Kloof Pass — the summit (touring map)

🚌 as (7a) above. On reaching the summit of the pass, park near a chain barrier across a gravel jeep track on the right (taking care not to block the entrance) and picnic nearby. *No walking, but see page 22:* you could walk along the track into the valley for a lovely outlook (1h or more).

7c Bain's Kloof Pass — Montagu Rocks (touring map)

🚌 as (7a) above. Halfway down the far side of the pass, the road goes past a high rocky outcrop on the right (the Montagu Rocks — 'Rots' in Afrikaans). There is a lay-by where you can park and a path to the top of the rock. This is wild country with some marvellous scenery. *No walking.*

8 Eastern slopes of Franschhoekpas (touring map)

🚌 Follow Car tour 5 to Franschhoek (page 27) and up the pass on the far side of town. There are several very scenic lay-bys on the left and one on the right after the right-hand hairpin bend near the summit. *No walking.*

9a Western slopes of Franschhoekpas: Jan Joubertsgatbrug (touring map)

🚌 Follow Car tour 5 to Franschhoek (page 27) and continue over the pass on the far side of town. After about 5km, park in a lay-by on the left, just before the road bends sharply to the left. Walk to the bend and cross the road (just before the road crosses the bridge). A path leads down to the stream underneath the bridge. Note the plaque describing the history of the bridge. *3min on foot.*

9b Western slopes of Franschhoekpas: Dutoitsrivier (touring map)

🚌 as (9a) above. A few hundred metres beyond the Jan Joubertsgatbrug, the road has been straightened to avoid a bend. Turn left here on the old road and park in the lay-by, to picnic overlooking the Dutoits River. *No walking.* The old road rejoins the new stretch on the far side of the bend.

10 Viljoenspas (touring map)

🚌 Follow Car tour 5 up Viljoenspas (page 29), to a large lay-by at a hairpin bend near the summit. The view extends over the Theewaterskloofdam and the mountains, rivers and orchards nearby. *No walking.*

11 Sir Lowry's Pass (touring map)

🚌 Follow Car tour 5 to the top of Sir Lowry's Pass (page 30). The lay-by on the left provides expansive views of False Bay, the peninsula and the nearby countryside. *No walking.*

12 Helderberg Nature Reserve (map page 105) 🚶

🚌 See Walk 19 (page 105) for access and full description, as well as short walks. The gardens *(a short stroll)* provide many tranquil picnic spots.

Picnic 6b: looking across the Cape flats to False Bay and the Kogelberge, from the summit of the Ou Kaapseweg

❀ Touring

These car tours are arranged so as to make the most of the area's attractions: the countryside with its mountains, orchards and vineyards, the picturesque towns and villages hidden away in the steep-sided valleys, the hospitality of town and country folk alike.

Because there is so much to see and experience, most of the tours have been kept quite short. There is little point in rushing through country like this, especially if you wish to take full advantage of the local hospitality. And there are very few areas in the world that rival this one on the latter score — or, for that matter, the quality of its food and wine.

And since this book is intended to be used in tandem with a standard guide, my touring notes are similarly brief. I concentrate instead on the 'logistics' of touring: times and distances, accurate route instructions, etc. Most of all, I emphasise the possibilities for **walking** and **picnicking**.

The fold-out touring map is designed to be held out opposite the touring notes, but its small scale limits the amount of detail which can be shown. I suggest that you also obtain a copy of the *Street guide* recommended on page 4: it covers most of the peninsula as well as other areas in the car tours. All the tours start in Rondebosch and are easily done in a day (except for Tour 5). The **distances** given are *cumulative* kilometres from the starting point. A key to the **symbols** in the text appears on the touring map.

Devil's Peak from the east-northeast

1 CAPE POINT

Rondebosch • Kirstenbosch • St James • Fish Hoek • Simon's Town • Cape Point • Scarborough • Ou Kaapseweg • Rondebosch

132km/82mi; about 3 hours' driving

On route: Picnics (see pages 8-9) (1), 2, (3), 4a, 4b, 6b; Walks 1-5, (9), 10-14, 16, (18)

This tour is a popular one, for obvious reasons, and the roads are very busy on weekends and in the high season. But on a weekday in cooler weather it is an outing not to be missed. The road passes close to both the peninsula's coastlines: False Bay to the east and the Atlantic to the west, the views all the way round providing constant feasts for the eye. The route chosen doesn't follow the main road initially; instead it leads to the settings for several walks , and quickly takes you off the beaten track.

Start from the fountain in the centre of Rondebosch: drive south along Main Road to the second set of traffic lights (not counting pedestrian crossings). Turn right into Klipper Road and follow it uphill and round to the left. It forks immediately: go left into Newlands Avenue and drive the whole length — to another set of traffic lights, beyond which you cross a dual carriageway: Union Avenue to the right and Paradise Road down to the left. *(The lay-by on Union Avenue marks the beginning of Walk 16.)*

You're now travelling along Rhodes Avenue which soon goes past the entrance to **Kirstenbosch★** (✿ The Botanical Gardens of South Africa) on the right. *(Walk 4 begins here, and the gardens are the setting for Picnic 2.)* The road then rises and arrives at a T-junction. Turn right and climb the next hill, with the gardens still on your right. The road swings sharp left at the top and passes the upper gate to Kirstenbosch (Rycroft Gate; 5km). *(This is where Walk 2 begins.)*

The road (now Rhodes Drive) then curls along the eastern skirts of Table Mountain, past Cecilia Forest. *(Park on the right here for Walk 3, or take the second turning left, to park at Bel Ombre for Picnic 3 or Walk 18.)* The road ends at Constantianek (9km 🍴✕🏠), where a small roundabout stands at the centre of a three-way junction. *(Walks 1 and 5 begin to the north of the roundabout.)* Up to this point the road has been sheltered by oaks, pines, chestnuts and gum trees for almost the entire way — one long winding avenue. As you turn left at the roundabout and descend another winding road (Main, the M41), the trees become even thicker, allowing only occasional glimpses of rambling gardens and white-walled houses on either side. (Note that at the bottom of the hill a signposted road goes right towards Groot Constantia (**M**), an early 19th-century house at the centre of the oldest vineyard in the country. It is a museum nowadays and contains an interesting collection of glassware, crockery, pictures and furniture. The junction is next to a rustic shopping complex with a 'farm-stall' selling an enormous variety of fresh and home-baked produce.)

After passing the junction, the road soon arrives at another set of traffic lights where you turn right into Ladies Mile Road. About 400m past yet another set of lights, turn right at a signpost to Muizenberg (15km) and join the 'Blue Route' — the Simon van der Stel Freeway. You've now joined the main route to the south (M3), a motorway which comes to an abrupt halt about 5km later. However, its brevity notwithstanding, the highway affords a fine view of the mountains over to the right: Vlakkenberg first and then Constantiaberg, with its TV mast reaching high above its summit. *(Access to Walk 9 is at the last junction on the motorway — the Tokai exit.)*

Turn left at the end of the motorway and drive down to a T-junction guarded by more lights, where you turn right on the old main road to the south. A few hundred metres later, in **Lakeside** (🚉), a road goes off right, at a junction which is signposted 'Boyes Drive' (22km). Follow the drive uphill and then to the left as it begins a long traverse across a range of mountains rising steeply up to the right. It is worth stopping at intervals along this road because it offers some of the best views of the drive: the lakes and water-

The lake in the centre of Kirstenbosch Gardens

ways north of **Muizenberg**, the long sweep of the northern shore of False Bay, and then the straggling seaside towns clinging one after the other to a narrow strip of land between the railway line and the mountains. In the far distance stand range upon range of mountains silhouetted against the eastern and northern skies. Some 5km along the drive you pass above **St James**. *(Walk 10 starts here.)*

Boyes Drive rejoins the coastal road after some 8km. Turn right and follow the road to **Fish Hoek** (*i*⚑✕🍴⊕) with its long sandy beaches and then to **Simon's Town** (40km *i*⚑✕🍴M) — famous for its naval harbour and maritime museums. Beyond Simon's Town the road continues along the western shores of False Bay in increasingly wild scenery until jagged mountains rising straight from the shore force it inland. Shortly afterwards, at the top of a steep winding rise, a well-signposted road turns left to the entrance of the **Cape of Good Hope Nature Reserve★** (53km), where you will be given a map of the reserve.

The narrow winding road (🎥🍴; photograph page 88) from the gate to the car park at Cape Point is 13km long — a 30 minute drive, due to the 40km speed limit. The speed restriction is designed to protect the reserve's game, including baboons, bontebok and tortoises (the latter being particularly vulnerable), so please drive slowly. *(Walk 14 begins at a lay-by about 500m beyond the gate, and the setting for Picnic 4a lies some 3.3km from the gate, on the right.)* The bigger mountains are behind you now, as the road wends its way down the peninsula's narrowing spine, the landscape on both sides of the road thick with subtly-changing *fynbos*. You pass several other roads going left and right to various points of interest on the way. (One of these is a circular drive going right: a worthwhile diversion, as it often reveals more of the animal and bird life in the reserve than the main route. See the map you were given at the gate.)

The main road comes to an end at a discreetly-hidden car park at **Cape Point★** (66km *i*✕🎥🍴M). *(Picnic 4b is close by.)* In fact, to give the architects their due, almost everything that's been built here is discreetly hidden. In creating a rare balance between modern man and his ancient environment, the authorities have gone a long way towards achieving what seems impossible almost everywhere else. The restaurants and shops, the litter bins and paths, the recently-built funicular railway: all of them have been landscaped with a commendable attention to detail. (So much so that it's almost impossible to find the toilets.)

In fact, if one can forgive the untruths about this being the meeting point of the Atlantic and Indian oceans and the over-enthusiastic use of the word 'historic', this is an experience to be savoured. The lighthouses, the enormous cliffs, the cormorants skimming across the sea, the tales of adventure, courage and maritime disaster: all play their part in an unforgettable scene.

There are various ways to return from the point: the one chosen has the advantage of being reasonably direct and scenic, but not so dramatic that it blurs the memory of Cape Point. It hugs the western shore instead of the eastern one. Turn left at the T-junction beyond the gate and follow the road for about 7km, then turn left again down a road signposted to **Scarborough** (90km). The town sprawls untidily by the sea, its disparate architecture clashing with the relentless waves at its feet. The road continues close to the shore for some time after leaving Scarborough, along a very rugged coastline, which appears to be in a permanent state of war with the thrashing ocean next to it.

Eventually, the road bends inland and arrives at another junction (97km). Turn right towards Fish Hoek, then go right again at the next T-junction. This road soon arrives at a crossroad where you turn left and go past the outskirts of Fish Hoek (105km). The road then becomes a mountain pass and carries you back over the peninsula's spine. This is the **Ou Kaapseweg** (Old Cape Road), a winding lane that requires care and concentration. *(Walk 11 starts at a large car park on the right-hand side of the road about 800m before the summit.)* The prospect from the top★ (☏) as you prepare to drive down the far side is quite exhilarating — a magnified panorama of the views obtained earlier in the day from Boyes Drive. *(You can turn left on a narrow road at the top, to the viewpoint shown on page 9 — the setting for Picnic 6b. This road also gives access to Walks 12 and 13 in the northern part of the Silvermine Nature Reserve.)*

After winding down from the pass, the road comes to a T-junction (116km) where you turn right and drive down to the Blue Route once more — 2km beyond the junction. Turn left on the motorway and head towards Cape Town. This time keep going along the motorway instead of turning off towards Constantianek. It eventually turns into a dual carriageway shortly before the outskirts of town, passing through three sets of traffic lights. At the fourth set of lights (the junction separating Newlands Avenue from Rhodes Avenue), turn right into Newlands Avenue and retrace your route back to Rondebosch (132km).

2 CHAPMAN'S PEAK DRIVE

Rondebosch • Cape Town • Llandudno • Hout Bay • Silvermine • Rondebosch

75km/47mi; 2 hours' driving (allow a full morning or afternoon)

On route: Picnics (see pages 8-9) (1), (5a, 5b, 5c), 6a, 6b; Walks 1, 5, (6), 7, 8, (15), (17)

This is one of the most spectacular tours in the Cape, its highlight an unforgettable drive along the precipitous western slopes of Chapman's Peak, high above the Atlantic. This section of road, connecting Hout Bay with the southern peninsula, was first completed in 1922 — a narrow gravel track cut into the sandstone. Since then the road has been widened and tarred, with crash barriers on one side — changes which have made the road a lot safer than it used to be. But the mountain itself hasn't been tamed: rocks still tumble down its flanks after heavy rain, and its deep gorges throw the road into a series of perilous contortions. These perils constitute a vital part of the route's attraction, of course, but there are plenty of other things to look at on the way round, including a remarkable view of Cape Town and the beaches along the Atlantic seaboard. Note that this tour can be driven just as easily the other way round but, if you do drive in a clockwise direction, take care on the Chapman's Peak section of the drive: the road travels very close to the edge of the cliff.

Start the drive from the centre of Rondebosch and follow Car tour 1 (page 11) until you get to the junction between Klipper Road and Newlands Avenue. Veer right here, instead of forking left, and follow the road uphill. *(Note the road to the Rhodes Memorial on the left as you approach Union Avenue: it leads to Walk 15 and Picnic 1.)* You join the arterial road leading into **Cape Town★** (*i*✝✿ ▲⌂✕♔⊕M☲); this urban motorway separates the older part of the university, lying on the slopes of Devil's Peak to the left, from more recent buildings down to the right.

Once past the university the road veers to the left and rises steadily past the hospital on the right and a sloping meadow to the left. Take the left fork (the M3) at the top of the hill and follow the road on its twisting way across the slopes of **Devil's Peak★**. There is a bird's-eye view of Cape Town from this section, straight across the city to Signal Hill and to the harbour and Table Bay further right. Some 8.5km from Rondebosch the road forks: the dual carriageway veers down to the right, but your road (M3) rises to the left. Keep going for about 1km to a set of traffic lights where you go over to the left-hand lane and drive straight ahead, instead of following the main road to the right.

This road arrives at a T-junction soon afterwards where you turn left on Upper Orange Street, which rises steeply towards Table Mountain. A few hundred metres up, a sign to the cableway points right, along Camp Road: take this turning and go through two sets of traffic lights. When the road ends at another T-junction, turn left again and drive

15

up Kloofnek Road — still following the signs to the cableway. This road is very steep and winding, eventually arriving at **Kloofnek** (), the saddle between **Table Mountain**★ and **Lion's Head**★. There is a small roundabout here where five roads converge. The road to the left goes to the cableway★ *(Picnics 5a and 5b);* the road to the right climbs Signal Hill *(Walk 17 and Picnic 5c;* photographs page 101). The fifth road, also to the right, descends to the sea at Clifton. You can, of course, stop wherever you like, for there is much to be seen and admired. Kloofnek stands high above the city on a narrow col between spectacular citadels of rock, the roads going left and right giving way to steadily-changing vistas of city, mountain and sea. In fact it is from viewpoints like these that you discover the secret of Cape Town's beauty — its setting.

The main tour, however, heads straight over the roundabout towards Camps Bay. The road veers left after a short distance and meanders downhill. *(Note the turning left to Fiskaal Road 2.5km beyond Kloofnek; it leads to Walk 6.)* After about 4.5km you meet the coastal road along the western shore of the peninsula (the M6; 17km). Turn left and follow it through **Camps Bay** (▲▲✕🍽) and out into the country. The road is close to the shore, scattered with rocky coves and stretches of white sand. High up to the left are the 'Twelve Apostles', a succession of prominent buttresses on the western escarpment of Table Mountain.

The road rises past the seaside resort of **Llandudno** before reaching another saddle between the southwestern corner of Table Mountain and a peak called **Little Lion's Head**★. *(At the beginning of the descent from this pass, note the sign to Suikerbossie on the left — the approach to Walk 7.)* The road descends to traffic lights on the outskirts of **Hout Bay** (*i*▲▲✕🍽M), a fishing town with an old harbour where fresh fish can be bought or eaten at a restaurant called The Mariner's Wharf. Fork left before the lights and travel for another kilometre, before arriving at another junction (26km), where you turn right. Now drive through the fringes of Hout Bay along a road which soon resumes its coastal character (still the M6).

The Twelve Apostles, on the descent from Kloofnek

The southern boundary of Hout Bay marks the start of **Chapman's Peak Drive★**, the peak itself appearing for the first time soon after the road begins to make its way steadily uphill. The drive is scenic from the word go, providing wonderful views of mountain and sea as it passes the remains of an 18th-century fort on the left (32km ■ 📷). There is an excellent view from this fort, across the bay to the Sentinel, the rocky peak guarding the entrance to the harbour. As the road (📷⌒) winds its way higher still, a notice appears on the left, warning of rockfalls. *(Walk 8 begins at the last right-hand bend before the top of the drive.)* At the crest★ (📷; *Picnic 6a;* photograph overleaf) there is a parking place on the right and a plaque giving a brief history of the road. The view from here is astonishing: the vast ocean rolling out to the western horizon, the mountains rising higher and higher to the north, and Hout Bay nestling behind its picturesque harbour in the foreground. And to the south, beyond the headland, the western face of Chapman's Peak comes into view for the first time, together with the line of your road winding across it. Above that curling line, red sandstone cliffs rise swiftly towards the sky, patched with lush green foliage, and far below, waves of white water splinter against the broken shore. The whole panorama is an unforgettable sight.

As the road continues down the far side of the hill, the greenery becomes less noticeable and the cliffs more sheer: gritty testimony to the courage and ingenuity of our hardy forebears. After passing several more lay-bys on the

way round the peak, the road pulls away from the coast and makes its way inland — opening out a view of the long and wide stretch of sand leading to the lighthouse at Kommetjie★. (There is a shipwreck buried about halfway along that beach: a steamer that came to grief on the nearby rocks many years ago. Scenes from the film *Ryan's Daughter* were shot there, before the sand almost engulfed the wreck.)

Beyond **Noordhoek** (✗) take the first *major* turning to the left after leaving the coast (signposted to Cape Town; 44km). Follow the road to its end 2km further on, then turn left on the Ou Kaapseweg (Old Cape Road; M64). This is the return route for Car tour 1: it crosses the **Silvermine** mountains before descending to the wide valley beyond them. If you haven't been this way before, the view from the top★ (📷) over False Bay to the distant mountains is both sudden and impressive — a prospect that seems to go on forever *(Picnic 6b;* photograph page 9*)*.

When you reach the foot of the pass on the far side, turn left and drive past the Steenberg Estate and through the Tokai Forest Reserve. Several kilometres beyond the forest the road reaches a set of traffic lights at Ladies Mile (60km). Turn left here and left again at the next set of lights about 1km further on. You're now travelling up the road to Constantianek instead of down it as in Car tour 1. As you climb higher, a really beautiful view★ of both Bel Ombre and the Eagle's Nest opens up above the trees. You come to a little roundabout at Constantianek (📷🍴). *(Walks 1 and 5 begin just to the north.)* The main tour turns right at this roundabout and returns to Rondebosch via the tree-lined avenues of Rhodes and Newlands (75km).

View to Hout Bay from the summit of Chapman's Peak Drive. The crest has been cleverly landscaped with paths and stone walls.

3 WEST COAST NATIONAL PARK

Rondebosch • Geelbeek • Postberg• Rondebosch

260km/161mi; 3 hours' driving

On route: ⩍ at Postberg and Geelbeek

The main aim of this tour is to visit the bird sanctuary at Geelbeek and the animal and flower park at Postberg. Both border the Langebaan Lagoon, a picturesque stretch of tidal water opening out to the Atlantic about 100km north of Cape Town. For once there are no mountains to look at, at least in the foreground — only low hills, coastal fynbos and water. September is the best month for the tour, when the migratory waterbirds start flying in from the north. It is also the only month when you can see the flowers at Postberg. The only restaurant is at the bird sanctuary, but there is no shortage of picnic places in both reserves. Several excellent hides have been built at the sanctuary from which you can observe the bird life, and in Postberg a network of roads and tracks passes close to the game. Choose a sunny day for the flowers, as most of them close their petals under cloud. And don't forget to take binoculars and a book on birds (see page 4).

To start the drive take the Black River Parkway (M5) out of Rondebosch — getting there via Belmont Road and Milner Road (which sweeps past the common). The parkway ends as it enters **Milnerton** (*i*▲✕🍴), where you turn left at the first set of traffic lights, following Section Road down to the coast road (R27). Turn right and follow the road as it passes a golf course to the left and then crosses a long bridge over a marsh and lagoon. After that the road soon shakes free of Cape Town's northern suburbs and heads north through undulating countryside.

There is not a great deal to look at along this road until you come to your turn-off to Geelbeek about 95km from Rondebosch (on the left and signposted '**West Coast National Park**'). At the gate, a few hundred metres from the junction, pick up maps and brochures and continue westwards. After about 9km along the tarred road, turn right on a gravelled jeep track signposted to Geelbeek.

The entrance to **Geelbeek★** (✕⩍) is on the left, about 2km beyond the turning. An access track leads to a car park next to a collection of farm buildings converted into a research centre. The countryside here is as flat as a pancake, low-lying and marshy, on the southern shore of the Langebaan Lagoon★. There are three hides within a reasonable walking distance of the car park — one to the north and two to the south. The northern one requires a walk along a jeep track for a few hundred metres and then another walk along a path to the left through increasingly marshy terrain. The path crosses a series of low wooden gangways; the last part of the path is screened from view. This hide is an extremely good one — large, and with 'windows' in all directions.

19

A similar journey to the south reveals two smaller hides dug into the ground, with more restricted views. But the birds seem to differ from one part of the reserve to another, so each hide has its advantages. All the hides are well signposted, and the restaurant and picnic tables next to the car park allow you to relax and compare notes. Among the hundreds of different birds to be seen in the reserve are various species of herons, storks, bitterns, pelicans, geese, ducks, coots, gulls, terns, godwits, plovers, sandpipers and oystercatchers. Some, like the curlew, rarely visit, while others congregate in large numbers. Flying pelicans are a wondrous sight to behold, circling round in stately formation, like squadrons of slow-moving but silent bombers — huge birds with enormous wingspans.

To find Postberg, drive back to the junction and turn right. The road now passes to the south of the lagoon, before turning north and travelling along its western shore. Large flocks of flamingoes are often to be seen near the water on the right-hand side of the road. After passing through the village of **Churchhaven** the road arrives at the entrance to **Postberg** (120km). An entrance fee is payable at the gate. In return you are given maps and details of the animals and birds to be found in this reserve. The game includes a wide variety of antelope, as well as zebra and a strange-looking animal called a bat-eared fox whose ears look like table tennis bats. The flowers are mostly vividly-coloured daisies. The roads inside Postberg are gravelled jeep tracks, one of which hugs the Atlantic coast for a while, sometimes well above it, sometimes just on the shore. There are one or two designated picnic places too (🖼🍴), one high up above the lagoon.

From Postberg take the same route back for about 60km. Then turn right on the M14 to **Melkbosstrand** (Milk-Bush Beach; ✕🍴), where you can head left on a road hugging the coast. Stop off at the southern end of **Bloubergstrand**

(Blue Mountain Beach; ▲▲✕🍴) and take a walk along the beach, to enjoy the outlook shown on page 4 — across Table Bay to Table Mountain and Lion's Head. This is the classic view★ of the mountain and harbour — the one seen from ships as they sail in from the north.

September at Postberg

4 THE NORTHERN BOLAND

Rondebosch • Paarl • Wellington • Bain's Kloof Pass • Wolseley • Tulbagh • Riebeek-Kasteel • Rondebosch

260km/161mi; 4 hours' driving

On route: Picnics (see pages 8-9) 7a, 7b, 7c

This is a long day's outing; start early to make the most of it. Make Tulbagh your lunchtime venue and take your time afterwards, driving back through some very attractive scenery in the late afternoon. There is much to be seen en route to Tulbagh, including the old market towns of Paarl and Wellington and the spectacular Bain's Kloof Pass. Eat at the Paddagang Restaurant in Tulbagh (after booking in advance), where you can experience the warmth of Boland hospitality in a truly memorable setting, with food and wine to match.

Drive from Rondebosch to the N1 motorway via the Black River Parkway (M5). Head for 'Paarl' on the motorway, and turn off on the R45 **Paarl** (60km *i*♟︎▲✕ ☎M). The street you have joined is one of the longest main streets in the country and is overlooked to the left by Paarl Mountain, a granite peak that glistens like a pearl *(paarl)* after rain. If you happen to drive this way very early in the morning, keep an eye on the rock: it sometimes emits a wisp of smoke near the top, where a runaway murderer once hid. His presence was betrayed by the smoke from his fire. He was hanged for his trouble, but people swear that the smoke from his cave still gives him away.

Vineyards lie at the side of the street, both right and left, encroaching all the way into the town. The huge building on the right, soon after passing the Laborie vineyards, is the head office of KWV, the company that controls much of the marketing and selling of South African wine. The street is also lined with many fine old oaks, as well as old houses and churches, some of the former dating back to the 18th century when the town was founded (1717). Keep to the main street as it wriggles through the centre and on towards Wellington.

Wellington (77km *i*♟︎☎) is much smaller than Paarl, with less shade in the summer heat. Founded in 1840, the town was given its name by Sir John Napier, then governor of the Cape, on the grounds that it was high time the duke's name appeared on the country's map! One of the country's leading Calvinist ministers, a Scotsman by the name of Andrew Murray, founded a seminary here in 1874. His statue stands in front of the church at the centre of town — to your left as you approach from Paarl. Your route goes right at the church and along the main street to the east (R303).

The town soon ends, giving way to rolling countryside and a steadily-rising road: **Bain's Kloof Pass★** (📷🗻), one

21

of many such roads built all over the Cape by another Scot called Andrew Geddes Bain, during the course of a long and industrious life in the 19th century. The narrow road winds slowly up to its summit, passing many picnic spots, some giving way to huge prospects to north and west *(Picnic 7a)*. At the summit (500m/1640ft) a gravel road with a chain across its entrance leads off to the right. You can park here and follow the track *(Picnic 7b)* for about 3km/2mi into a beautiful valley flanked by high mountains. A monument on the left of the track commemorates a tragedy that occurred here over a century ago, when a party of girls from the seminary was stranded by the swollen waters of the Witrivier (White River). They were on their way back from climbing Klein Wellington, a huge dome 1600m/5248ft high. One of the girls and three of her would-be rescuers were drowned; the rest were rescued later. The ruins of an old house lie further to the right. The valley and the river-bank to its left make beautiful picnic spots.

The road passes a jumble of tumbledown buildings at the top of the pass, before winding its way down the far side alongside the Witrivier, which dashes down a rock-strewn bed far below. This is magnificent country, especially on a fine day when the sun picks out the subtle greys, greens and browns of the savage scenery all around you. Just under halfway down you pass a spectacular picnic setting at the Montagu Rocks★ (⌧; *Picnic 7c)*. Then the road passes under an overhanging rock, Dacre's Pulpit, where a clergyman of that name blessed the pass when it was opened in 1853. From the bottom of the pass follow the R303 until it joins the R43 some 29km beyond Wellington. The road then continues to **Wolseley** (121km ⌧), a small town that your growing appetite may render all but invisible.

Soon after passing through Wolseley turn left towards Tulbagh, your luncheon venue. (An alternative plan of course is to picnic en route and have tea in Tulbagh instead — the Paddagang Restaurant is open until 5pm.) The area round **Tulbagh** (137km *i*⌧⌧⌧M⌧) was first settled in the 1700s, when a vineyard was started to the west of the present town in 1710: De Twee Jonge Gezellen (The Two Young Batchelors). It has remained in the hands of the same family ever since — the founders having given up their bachelorhood once their fortunes improved. However, the town was only given its name in 1804 (after the governor of the time, Ryk Tulbagh). The old main street at its centre (defended by numerous sleeping policemen) is full of interesting buildings which had to be restored after

Countryside near Malmesbury, with Table Mountain in the distance

a devastating earthquake in 1969. The Paddagang Restaurant lies on the left-hand side of the street behind green lawns and shrubs sloping down from the road. Paddagang means 'frog's way' — presumably because the many marshes in the area were (and still are) havens for frogs. The building, a white-walled farm with a thatched roof, is hung with cartoons of frogs inside, but its tables — both inside and out — are mostly laden with local foods such as *waterblommetjie* and *bobotie,* Dutch and Malay delicacies whose chief ingredients are edible water flowers, curried lamb, rice and spiced butternut.

Possible detours (not in the total distance). At the end of the main street, you could take a wide road off left (west) to De Twee Jonge Gezellen, about 6km away. This picturesque collection of buildings, set among trees and lawns, is well worth a visit. Or, if you turn right at the end of the street instead of left, and then go left immediately beyond the *pastorie* (parsonage), you would come to another vineyard some 3km from town: the Drostdyhof (**M**). The old house is now a museum containing some fine furniture. Tulbagh and its vineyards are sheltered by high mountains to the north and northwest, including the Klein and Groot Winterhoek peaks (1619m/5310ft and 2078m/6816ft) which can be seen to advantage from Drostdyhof — over to the west, the latter behind the former.

After leaving Tulbagh take the R46 signposted to Gouda and drive through the Nuwekloofpas to the west. Follow the R44 towards Hermon and then turn right on the R46 to **Riebeek-Kasteel** (167km 🍴🏪🎦). This is a beautiful little town, full of fruitful gardens and trees, with a lovely church at its centre. Stick to the R46 as you go through town, a road that eventually reaches the outskirts of **Malmesbury** (183km). Turn left here on the N7, a dual carriageway that by-passes the town and crosses the R315 over a high bridge. From there drive south until the road reaches the N1 (243km), where you return to Rondebosch the way you came (260km).

5 THE FOUR PASSES

Rondebosch • Stellenbosch • Helshoogtepas • Fransch hoek • Franschhoekpas • Theewaterskloofdam • Vil joenspas • Sir Lowry's Pass • (Helderberg) • Rondebosch

*183km/113mi; only 3 hours' driving, but **allow two days***

On route: Picnics (see pages 8-9) 8, 9a, 9b, 10, 11, (12); Walks (19, 20) 21, (22-23)

This tour is really two tours in one. There is so much to see and experience en route that scant justice can be done to the drive in one day. In parti cular, both Stellenbosch and Franschhoek are towns of great historica and gastronomic interest, with fruitful vineyards and glorious mountai scenery on their doorsteps. So, if you have enough time, arrange a visit to Stellenbosch on one day and Franschhoek on another. The drive i particularly beautiful in the spring, when the fruit trees are in blossom, bu an autumn visit is rewarding too, when the trees and vines are dressed i all sorts of fiery colours and the orchards are laden with fruit. While the Helderberg is easily reached from this tour, I recommend you devote full day to the nature reserve (Picnic 12, Walks 19 and 20; see page 105)

To start the drive from Rondebosch, make for the N2 Motorway via Belmont Road and the Liesbeek Parkway. Keep driving eastwards along the N2 until you reach the Stellenbosch and Eersterivier turn-off (R310) about 28km from Rondebosch. Turn left and follow the road towards Stellenbosch. On the way it passes several vineyards, including one called Spier (✕) which now houses an open-air concert platform and has its own railway station nearby. Soon after passing the Spier Winery, the road crosses the railway line, about 100m past a sign to the Van Ryn Brandy Cellars on the right-hand side of the road. These cellars are worth a visit. They form part of a 'Brandy Route', designed to familiarise tourists with the history and skills behind the distilling process. One of the trades still practised here is the cooper's — a handcraft of remarkable precision.

After crossing the railway bridge, the road continues through the village of **Vlottenburg** and joins a dual-carriageway road into Stellenbosch. A fountain, marking the entrance to the Neethlingshof Vineyard, throws water high into the air on the opposite side of the road at the junction. Shortly after entering **Stellenbosch★** (40km *i*⚲ ▲✕🅿M), the road (still the R310) passes a large pond on the right, inhabited by hundreds of waterbirds — a rustic feature which soon gives way to the Stellenbosch Farmers' Winery, its high fence covered from top to tail with brilliant red and purple bougainvillea. On the other side of the road, beyond the entrance to the winery, lies a vineyard bor-dered by roses. The Oude Libertas Theatre — an open-air amphitheatre offering a wide variety of concerts and plays on summer weekends — is hidden in a copse of trees

24

behind these vines. These buildings are part of modern Stellenbosch, low-lying suburbs which have spread out from the old town; the latter founded in 1779 by one of the Cape's early governors, Simon van der Stel.

But before going any further, a word or two about the town's setting — which can hardly have escaped your attention long before passing the duck pond! The scenery in which the original settlers chose to build Stellenbosch is unforgettable, totally stunning. The mountains brooding over the town's wooded streets and church steeples form a high alpine arc under the drama of an African sky. From Helderberg in the east to Simonsberg to the northwest, the horizon is filled with towering peaks in a steep kaleidoscope of light and shade. And beneath these sleeping giants, hills and valleys roll down to the sea, quilted with orchards, forests and vineyards. The sleepiness of the scene is deceptive too, for town and countryside harbour one of the most successful businesses in South Africa: the fruit and wine industry, whose markets straddle the world. So the hospitality for which the Boland is deservedly famous is based on something more than mere goodwill; there's nothing like prosperity for widening the smile.

One of the easiest ways of exploring Stellenbosch is to turn right at the first set of traffic lights after the road has passed the winery and recrossed the railway line. The turning leads to Dorp Street, the oldest in town and lined with oak trees descended from those planted by van der Stel 300 years ago. The street is lined with some fascinating old houses, many with preservation orders. Park on the Drostdy by the Modder Kerk at the top end of the street on the left. There are many buildings to look at, including the church at your side and a costume and furniture museum to the left of the church. (The museum is one of several depicting the lives of the old Dutch settlers and their more well-to-do descendants. These museums give some fascinating insights into early European life too — insights not often uncovered in the 'old world'.) There is an information centre nearby, halfway down Plein Street, on the right, where you can get all the brochures and maps you need. And, of course, there is a plentiful supply of restaurants and pavement coffee-houses in the centre of town and on the outskirts. If you are spending the day in Stellenbosch rather than going on to Franschhoek, try the Lanzerac Hotel for afternoon tea; it is set in outstanding scenery and has recently recovered some of its former glory. (Continue up Dorp Street, and you will find it signposted.)

Bothmaskop, at the first of the four passes — Helshoogte (Heights of Hell), near Stellenbosch

If you intend restricting your day to Stellenbosch and the surrounding countryside, take the R304 out of town and drive for about 8km before turning left on the M23. This road passes several wineries on its way back to Cape Town via Kuilsrivier. When you meet a T-junction after another 15km, turn left and then left again at a major junction controlled by traffic lights. Keep to the right on a busy dual carriageway between Kuilsrivier and Bellville, then turn right on the R300, a motorway which leads back to the N2 (about 12km to the south). Keep a sharp look-out for the exit to the N2, a major interchange with large signposts pointing the way to Somerset West and Cape Town. Take the Cape Town slip road onto the N2 and return to Rondebosch by your outward route. This interchange won an architectural award; it is a remarkably slender design, best appreciated when driving beneath it.

If you are continuing to Franschhoek from Stellenbosch, head northeast on the R310. *(Note that the turning to the right after the traffic lights outside the town leads to Walks 22 and 23.)* Now climb steadily to the top of the first of the four passes, **Helshoogtepas★**. This is majestic country, the road sweeping over the lower slopes of Bothmaskop (914m/2998ft) in a series of long loops as it approaches the neck between the *kop* and its lofty neighbour, Simonsberg, standing well to the left. The latter (see pages 28-29) dominates the landscape between Stellenbosch and Paarl: its six razor-like peaks —the highest 1390m/4600ft above sea level — form a reptilian spine of gargantuan proportions. A cluster of vineyards lies at the top of the pass, where the road swings right and enters the Drakensteinvallei (Valley of the Dragons of Stone). It was Simon van der Stel who gave this valley its name in 1687, after he'd travelled there in order to formalize its status in the colony and allocate farmland for settlement. The name commemorated the 1685 visit of Hendrick Adriaan Drakenstein, the company's commissioner-general. A more appropriate name could not be imagined. Not only does the rocky north-eastern face of Simonsberg overlook it from one side, but further ahead to the right lies an even more massive range of mountains: Groot-Drakenstein. This range presents an

26

awesome face to the traveller from any direction, particularly from the top of the pass, when shafts of sunlight pick out the lines of the huge buttresses in savage detail.

The road passes to the left of these mountains, through the villages of **Johannesdal** (🚆) and **Pniel** (🚆), shortly reaching Boschendal (✖M), over to the right. The outbuildings of this old house form part of the wine estate in which the manor resides, the ones near the house containing a shop and a couple of restaurants. One of the latter serves excellent help-yourself lunches in a long barn, while hampers provided by the winery can be eaten on the lawns during summer. Booking is essential: telephone 8741252.

The R310 ends a couple of kilometres past Boschendal, after crossing a railway line. Turn right at the junction and follow the R45 towards Franschhoek. This road continues travelling the Drakenstein Valley in an easterly direction, with the Groot-Drakenstein range of mountains on the right and the Klein-Drakenstein range on the left. This part of the valley is full of vineyards and orchards, many with French names dating back to the early days of Huguenot settlement. The road also crosses the Bergrivier where canoe races are run further downstream every year.

Franschhoek★ (70km *i*🛏✖🚆M) lies at the eastern end of the valley. Its name means 'French Corner', a literal

The Groot-Drakenstein range rises over vineyards near Franschhoek. This town is a gourmet's delight. In keeping with the Huguenot influence, nearly all the restaurants have French names — and several serve excellent French food as well as the local dishes. Among many others, Le Quartier Français, Chez Michel, Le Ballon Rouge, La Maison de Chamonix and La Petite Ferme have proved their quality over time.

translation from the Huguenot *Le Quartier Français*. The Huguenot influence is everywhere. Apart from sampling the superb French and local cuisine and a host of vineyards, you can visit a fine museum depicting the life and times of the Huguenot settlers (at the far end of town, to the left of the gardens at the end of the main road).

The next stage of the route goes left at the T-junction in front of the gardens and starts ascending the second of the four passes: **Franschhoekpas★**. This one is no less spectacular than Helshoogte, rising along the western slopes of Middagskransberg (literally Noon-Cliff Mountain) to a saddle overlooking a veritable feast of highland scenery. The entrance to La Petite Ferme lies a short way along this road, where there are also many lay-bys (📷) from which to admire the view and picnic — both on the way up *(Picnic 8)* and on the way down the far side. The summit of this pass stands some 700m/2300ft above sea level (against Helshoogte's 400m/1300ft), occupying a lofty seat in the middle of this fantastic table. Five major ranges are spread out within a wide circle: Groot-Drakenstein to the west, Klein-Drakenstein at your feet to the north, Wemmershoekberge further north and east, Aasvoelberge (Mountains of the Vultures) to the southeast and Franschhoekberge close behind you to the south. Several of the higher peaks are frequent hosts to winter snows. A track cuts back left here at the summit, and you can picnic at various places alongside it; the track ends at a closed gate a few hundred metres from the road. *(Walk 21 starts at this gate.)*

From the top of the pass the road sweeps down a long valley flanked by the Wemmershoekberge to the left and Franschhoekberge to the right. After about 5km the road crosses a stone bridge (Jan Joubertsgatbrug); it was constructed in 1823 and has since been hidden by the new road — at a hairpin bend to the left. A path leads down to the old bridge (📷; *Picnic 9a*) from the road, opposite a lay-by on the left. Shortly after crossing the bridge, the road bypasses a gravel track on the left — part of the old road. The track, a short loop, provides a bird's-eye view of the gorge at the centre of the valley (📷; *Picnic 9b*). The Dutoitsrivier, flowing through the rocks far below, starts its life only a short distance away in the Klein-Drakensteinberge

Pniel church, with Simonsberg rising behind it

and is a fine sight after rain. The road soon reaches the bottom of the valley and makes its way past a huge reservoir: the **Theewaterskloofdam**, Cape Town's chief source of water. The R45 ends soon afterwards, reaching the R310 at a T-junction: turn right here and make your way across the middle of the reservoir over a long bridge.

As the road continues south across a broad and fertile plain, the shores of the reservoir gradually recede, replaced by growing numbers of orchards. This valley and the valley beyond the next pass (Viljoenspas) form the heart of the Boland's fruit industry. Thousands upon thousands of trees, bearing apples, pears, peaches and apricots grow in thick profusion on both sides of the road. In springtime the countryside is alive with white and pink blossom, and the streams, rivers and dams are full to the brim: a veritable Garden of Eden.

Viljoenspas★ is only a few kilometres beyond Theewaterskloofdam. A hairpin bend going left near its summit provides another picnic spot (📷; *Picnic 10*) and another viewpoint over the Theewaterskloof valley. The sleek river below is Riviersonderend (River-Without-End), so named by the Dutch settlers because it seemed to go on forever as they sought new pastures further east. Its course is now interrupted by the Theewaterskloofdam, but it still continues for many kilometres along the southern flank of the desolate Riviersonderendeberge before joining the Breederivier near Swellendam. The combined rivers eventually empty out into the warm waters of the Indian Ocean beyond Cape Aghulas.

The journey through the Elgin valley on the far side of the pass is even more picturesque, the road undulating through fields of orchards overlooked by the Groenland- berge to the east and the Hottentots-Holland mountains to the west. The road comes to an end in the town of **Elgin** (121km 🚩). There is a choice of routes here, left or right. Both routes take you to the N2 road to Cape Town — the road to the right going through the unremarkable town of Grabouw on the way. There are farm stalls on both roads where they join the N2 — an advantage if you're catering for yourself.

The last of the four passes, **Sir Lowry's Pass★**, lies on the N2 about 12km west of Grabouw. The summit is reached shortly after the road rises to the left after crossing a half- hidden reservoir called Upper Steenbras Dam. There is a large car park at the top, on the left, sheltered from the road by a large outcrop of rock (📷; *Picnic 11*). This pass was built in 1828 and named after the governor of the time, Sir Lowry Cole; it replaced a more primitive oxen track (Gantouwpas) that climbed straight up the mountainside further inland. The road has been widened several times since then, and cantilevered near the top where the railway line passes under it, but the distant view remains largely unaltered: it is colossal. From this vantage point, some 456m/1485ft above sea level, you are looking across the full sweep of False Bay, right across to the Cape Peninsula, which for all its distance stands out clearly on the western horizon — the whole length of it from north to south. In the foreground to your right, the rocky buttresses of the Hottentots-Holland mountains rise sharply in the after- noon light. And in front of you, the eight peaks of the Helderberg (Clear Mountain) look down on the hilly countryside surrounding Somerset West. A thin white line of skyscrapers marks Strand's beachfront on the bay's northern shore. If you time things right you may be lucky enough to reach the top of the pass at sunset, when the sky is wreathed in variegated clouds, the western horizon deepening into a rich shade of red as the sun sinks below the peninsula's silhouette.

The journey from the top of the pass to Rondebosch is just over 50km. (*Access to Picnic 12 and Walks 19 and 20 is at the Strand exit, some 12km along, but the Helderberg Nature Reserve deserves a full day of your visit.*) Return the way you came, leaving the N2 at the Liesbeek Parkway junction and turning right into Belmont Road at the third set of traffic lights — at the top of a long rise.

 Walking

Twenty-three main walks are described in this book, together with a number of options for each. The bulk of the walks are on Table Mountain and the Cape Peninsula, the rest further along the southern coast or in the interior: the Boland. Although the descriptions of the short and alternative walks are brief, these options have been chosen carefully — many are almost as challenging as the main walks and just as interesting.

Access

Although there are trains and buses running up and down the peninsula, for the most part they do not get you close enough to the walk starting point to be practical. For this reason, all the walks have been written up with **access by car** from Rondebosch, a suburb some 10km south of Cape Town. It is a convenient centre from several points of view — not least its proximity to both mountain and town. For ease of reference, all the walks are keyed into the car tours, which also start at Rondebosch.

However, it *is* possible to reach a couple of the walks by public transport. You could get to St James (Walk 10) by **train** (frequent services; tel: 405 3871). There are also **buses** from Wynberg Station to Hout Bay via Constantianek, giving access to Walks 1 and 5 (tel: 080121 2111).

Guides, waymarking, maps

Note that **guides** are available for the more ambitious walks. There are several excellent professional guides in Cape Town, including Richard Behne (448 6359), Oliver Dolby (083255 3466), Leonhard Rust (685 5897), Ross Suter (478036) and Euan Waugh (797 3386). On a more informal basis, the writer can be contacted on 797 1731.

The paths in Kirstenbosch and on sections of Table Mountain and Helderberg are well signposted, but elsewhere **waymarking** is infrequent and you will have to rely on the maps and notes in this book.

The **walking maps** are drawn to a scale of 1:40,000, except for the 1:13,000 map on the reverse of the touring map. All of them are based on Chief Directorate of Surveys and Mapping 1981-1984 maps, updated where necessary. The writer has walked almost all of the paths shown on the maps many times, in an attempt to map them properly, but complete accuracy cannot be guaranteed. Also, please note that *in the interests of preserving the natural beauty of the mountains, only the main paths are followed in the walks.* Other paths have been drawn in for navigational purposes only: the necessary resources just aren't available to maintain them in good order. *Please, therefore, stick to the paths described in this book — those highlighted in green.*

Weather

The walks are set out *according to the seasons,* as well as geographically. All the walks in the book can be tackled during autumn, winter and spring, but the Boland in particular should be avoided altogether in summer (early November to mid-April): it is far too hot for most people at that time of the year. To be more specific:

- Walks 1-4 can be done all the year round, given a coolish day, and they are right on your doorstep.
- Walks 5-8 can be undertaken in summer, provided that you set out early and the day's weather forecast predicts warm (rather than *hot*) weather.
- Walks 9-18 are best avoided in summer.
- Walks 19-23 should be avoided at all costs in summer, especially Walks 22 and 23.

Another point to bear in mind is that, contrary to popular belief, winter days (mid-June to mid-August) are often clear and still, the bulk of the rain falling overnight. The weather in spring and autumn is more unpredictable, but the atmosphere and colours at those times of the year are really beautiful — well worth the wait for a fine day. *(But no matter how little time you have, avoid walking in the rain: temperatures can drop dramatically in the mountains, even in summer).*

Nuisances

Dogs are not a hazard, nor are **snakes**; the latter are rarely encountered and usually move away when approached. The best way to avoid snakes is to stay off the mountains in hot weather and to avoid the Boland walks altogether from November to March. If you are allergic to **insect bites**, be sure to keep the necessary medication with you in your first-aid kit. Inspect your body for **ticks** after a walk, especially if the latter involves brushing through thick undergrowth; see a doctor if a bite begins to swell. If you meet a troop of **baboons**, give them the right of way. Nine times out of ten they'll give you a wide berth anyway.

*Watch out for **bushes with pale serrated leaves**. Two in particular can cause skin rashes: the blister bush (shown right) and Smodingium argutum. The poison is activated by sunlight, and it may take some time before the rash appears. It can be treated with a cortisone cream.*

Only when fed by their silly human cousins are they likely to become a nuisance.

What to take

Make sure you've packed enough clothing and equipment *for all four seasons,* no matter what time of year you visit. The weather can always change suddenly in mountainous country, and the Cape is no exception. Note the following as well:

- The terrain is hard on the feet: **strong and comfortable boots** with well-cushioned soles and good ankle support are better than any other kind of footwear on these paths — and more economical in the long run. But there is no need to go to the expense of buying hiking boots if you intend sticking to the shorter options.
- Wear **two pairs of socks** inside your boots — to prevent blisters and provide additional cushioning.
- Most of the time **shorts are better than long trousers** — particularly in wet weather when the latter take a long time to dry. The important thing is to keep your torso warm, as it acts as the body's boiler.
- On a warm and sunny day remember to take a **broad-rimmed hat and suncream**, even when there are clouds about.
- The skin on your arms is more susceptible to burning than the skin on your legs. Wear a cotton or similar **long-sleeved shirt** in sunny weather and keep your legs covered with suncream, particularly behind and above the knees.
- Take a **whistle** with you. It saves the breath needed to curse your ill luck when you're lost or injured. And don't forget the **first-aid kit**.

Walkers' checklist

Before you start walking in the Cape, take it easy for a few days after the long flight. Then start with one of the easier walks in the book (Walk 1 is ideal). Your walks will be all the more enjoyable if you observe a few basic rules, especially when undertaking the more strenuous hikes.

- **Plan your routes in advance** and allow ample time to finish in daylight.
- Bear in mind that it is easier to **keep to a slow rhythm** when walking uphill rather than constantly changing pace as the gradient steepens and eases. The same applies on the descents.
- **If you lose your way**, retrace your steps to the last known landmark and start again. Don't plough on regardless, and don't descend on an unknown path unless you can see its route all the way down.
- When you stop for lunch on a cold day, **put on extra clothing** straight-away. Don't wait until you start feeling cold: by then it's too late.

- **If the weather looks as though it will turn nasty**, return as quickly a: possible and put protective clothing on before the rain overtakes you

- **Eat in the shade** *and keep drinking water — a litre every two hour in warm weather.*

- If you start feeling tired for no apparent reason — probably on a hc day — you're not drinking enough (the first signs of **dehydration**).

- If any of your party is showing signs of **hypothermia** (bouts of shiver ing, slow reactions, slurred speech) get him or her off the mountain a: quickly as possible. It's essential to keep dry and to wear warn clothing underneath your waterproofs. Heavy rain reduces the tem perature very quickly.

- If **cramp** overtakes you, drink as much water as you can. Anothe remedy is 'lemon twist', a soft drink containing the appropriate pro portion of quinine. It can be purchased at most supermarkets anc corner cafés. Dolomite, Magnesit and Slow-Mag tablets also preven cramp as they both contain plenty of magnesium, a commodity ir short supply in South African soil. However, to be effective they have to be taken beforehand.

- Avoid going for long walks with fewer than three people and *neve** walk alone.* Leave a note with a responsible person describing exactly where you are going and when you expect to be back.

Country code

C I hope the 'Walkers' checklist' above helps you avoic any unpleasant misadventures on your walks. Please help us, too, to protect our precious environment.

- **Stick to the paths described**. The zigzags are designed to protect the terrain from erosion. Do not use short cuts.

- **Do not light fires**, except at approved barbecue sites.

- **Do not pick flowers or disturb animals and birds.**

- **Take all your litter away with you.**

- **Obtain permits** (before setting out) where indicated in the book.

- **Do not enter private property** even if it looks abandoned.

- **Respect everyone's right to peace and quiet.**

Organisation of the walks

O Each of the walks is described as **easy, moderate** or **strenuous**, the grades largely depending on the steepness of the terrain and the length of the walk. The **walking times** given are based on the unhurried pace of a group of four reasonably-experienced hikers. It shouldn't take long to discover how they fit in with your particular pace. Below is a key to the **symbols** on the walking maps.

▬▬▬ dual carriageway	🚗 car parking	■ ▫ building/ruin
▬▬ main road	🚉 train station	● rock
▬ secondary road	*P* recommended picnic	▲ hotel
▬ track	🚩 picnic tables	🕱 transmitter
------ footpath	📷 best views	⋂ cave
4 ➤ main walk	894 peak and height	† cross
4 ➤ alternative	▲ in metres	🗡 waterfall, spring
	▮ castle	🔸 river/pool

1 TABLE MOUNTAIN CONTOUR PATH FROM CONSTANTIANEK TO THE RHODES MEMORIAL

Map begins on page 52, continues on the map inside the back cover, and ends on page 93; see photographs pages 12 and 94

Distance/time: 11km/6.8mi; 3h30min

Grade: easy, as its name implies, though the terrain is very rocky in places and there is a steep rise and fall about halfway along, just after the path clears the Kirstenbosch Botanical Gardens. Climb 270m/885ft.

Equipment: boots or stout walking shoes, jersey, waterproofs, sunhat, picnic, plenty of water. The walk is shady enough not to need special precautions in summer — except for a sunhat.

How to get there and return: 🚌 bus from Wynberg railway station (four stops south of Rondebosch) to Hout Bay; get off at Constantianek. Walk back to Rondebosch from the finishing point at the Rhodes Memorial. 🚗 leave one car at the Rhodes Memorial and another at Constantianek. The journey by car from Rondebosch to the *nek* is about 9.5km and follows the route described in Car tour 1 on page 11. Park in the open area on the north side of the roundabout, on the opposite side from the restaurant. See Car tour 2, page 15, for location of the Rhodes Memorial.

Alternative walks

1 Kirstenbosch Gardens. Any time after the Contour Path enters Kirstenbosch, there are various other paths leading down into the gardens. Once you're there, a rudimentary sense of direction and a plethora of good signposts will ensure you don't lose sight of the Contour Path, your lifeline back to Constantianek. These walks are similar in length to the main walk and are easily accomplished in walking shoes. As there is virtually no shade in the gardens, be sure to take a sunhat in summer.

2 Cecilia Forest circuit from Constantianek. 5km/3mi; 1h15min; easy; access/return by 🚌 or 🚗 to/from Constantianek (as above). Walking shoes adequate, but take sunhat and suncream in summer, as the return path is exposed to the sun. Follow the main walk to the large gum tree (36min), double back right for a few metres/yards on the lower jeep track, and then peel off left down a path. After about 300m/yds the path — running down alongside a stream to its left — drops on to another jeep track where you turn right and follow it past three other jeep tracks, one coming in from the right, another doubling back to the left, and the third doubling back to the right. The track then winds in and out of several deep gullies before forking right and rejoining the Contour Path 9min from your starting point. Follow the Contour Path back to Constantianek.

This walk, known simply as the Contour Path, is a real beauty, an ideal introduction to both the Cape and Table Mountain — far better this way than flinging oneself at the mountain from the word go. The scenery changes slowly and subtly as the walk progresses, its quiet atmosphere cooling the mind almost from the beginning.

Table Mountain richly deserves the accolades that have been heaped upon its sturdy shoulders over the years — whether by passing mariners, awestruck visitors or parochial Capetonians. To begin with, its credentials go back a long way. Geologists place its birth some 280 million years ago — a massive chunk of granite, shale and sandstone gradually rising above the surface of the sea over many

35

millions of years. There it has remained ever since, together with the peninsula chain of mountains to the south, shaped and reshaped by wind, rain and avalanche, dominating the skyline for many miles around. At first sight the mountain looks better suited to climbing than walking; its lofty summit, 1086m/3560ft high, is guarded on three sides by formidable cliffs and buttresses rising almost sheer from the thickly-foliaged slopes below. But there are plenty of paths between those cliffs, particularly on the southern side of the mountain — the 'Back Table', where the terrain is less harsh than on the 'Front Table' above it.

This walk travels northwards across the eastern slopes of both Table Mountain and its northern neighbour, Devil's Peak, starting in the pine and gum plantations of Cecilia Forest at the southern end of Table Mountain, passing above the Botanical Gardens of South Africa, Kirstenbosch, and finishing on the far side of Newlands Forest, on the lower slopes of Devil's Peak. The starting point is 215m/705ft above sea level, rising to 480m/1575ft about halfway along and descending to 160m/525ft at the Rhodes Memorial.

To begin the walk, take the right-hand tarred drive running north from the parking area north of Constantia-nek. The drive (lined with trees to the left and houses with large gardens to the right) ends at a gate about 300m/yds from the *nek*. Beyond the gate the road becomes a jeep track, soon entering Cecilia Forest. Some 40m/yds along, the path taken in Walk 5 climbs up to the left, but keep ahead on the jeep track. After **9min** the track forks; go left and follow the track steadily uphill. Continue through the trees for some distance, passing two widely-spaced jeep tracks on the left and then another coming in at an acute angle from the right. This three-way junction, in Cecilia Ravine, is guarded by the last and biggest of a row of large gum trees (**36min**). *(Alternative walk 2 turns back here.)* Now referring to the map inside the back cover, follow the track northwards for a short distance until it peters out into a path — which soon clambers up to the left over a series of steps (**45min**).

At the top of the rise the path emerges from the forest into Kirstenbosch, where a signpost points the way north along the Contour Path and to various other points of the compass, including the cultivated sections of the gardens down to the right *(Alternative walk 1)*. From here, at last, the woods can be seen separated from the trees — and a fine sight they are too, sweeping across the mountainside ahead (Newlands Forest). The eastern flank of the Back

Table slopes steeply up to the left, covered in a picturesque mixture of thick *fynbos* and rock.

The path continues above the gardens for a kilometre or more, passing several downward paths, the long view interrupted halfway along by the trees and bushes lining Nursery Ravine and vanishing altogether as the path enters Skeleton Gorge. Both gorges descend steeply from the top of the Back Table, carrying swiftly-flowing water into the gardens below. In fact, Skeleton Gorge is a sight for sore eyes after heavy rain, when a wide waterfall dashes down the mossy slabs of rock lying just above the path (sometimes making the crossing a little hazardous). Shortly after navigating another dark ravine (Window Gorge), the path forks left and starts to climb in earnest (**1h30min**), rising some 250m/820ft to a fine viewpoint on heavy scree brought down from Fernwood Buttress high up to the left.

After crossing the scree the path descends again to a large rock on the right, in dark woodland (**2h**). This is where the path officially enters Newlands Forest, although it has scarcely seen the light of day since entering Skeleton Gorge. (*This rock also marks the last path down to Kirstenbosch for those who wish to return to Constantianek via the gardens. But this particular path is not very easy to follow; most of it is explored in the first part of Walk 2.*)

From here on the main route is straightforward, every signpost pointing the way to the Rhodes Memorial. The route continues north through thick woodland, with occasional openings in the canopy of leaves revealing dramatic glimpses of the towering walls and buttresses of the Top Table high above — and wide open country to the eastern horizon. There is a broad path leading down to Newlands part-way along (**2h30min**) and then another heavy rock-scree at the base of Newlands Ravine — the latter rising out of sight to a high saddle between Table Mountain and Devil's Peak on the left. A few hundred paces beyond the scree, the Newlands Ravine path branches off left. The Contour Path then continues north through the forest for another 2km (map page 93) before emerging on the open slopes of Devil's Peak at the second of two turnstiles set about 1.5km apart (**3h10min**). The car park next to the Rhodes Memorial can be seen from here.

The walk leaves the Contour Path here, descending sharply to the right a few metres before the turnstile. You cross two jeep tracks en route. This section is heavily used and badly eroded in places and needs some care in wet weather. The descent takes about 20 minutes (**3h30min**).

2 KIRSTENBOSCH AND NEWLANDS FOREST FIGURE-OF-EIGHT

See map inside back cover; see also photographs pages 12, 48-49

Distance/time: 10km/6.2mi; 3h05min

Grade: moderate, although it can become strenuous if rushed — an easy mistake to make in this sort of terrain. The path undulates throughout, making it difficult to find a decent walking rhythm. Climb 270m/885ft.

Equipment: boots or sturdy shoes, jersey, waterproofs, sunhat, picnic, water; suncream and long-sleeved shirt in sunny weather

How to get there and return: 🚌 to/from the top (Rycroft) gate at Kirstenbosch (follow Car tour 1 on page 11); park at the side of the road opposite the gate. *Note that a small entrance fee is payable at the gate.*

Short walks: each loop of the figure-of-eight can be done separately.

1   Kirstenbosch. 4.5km/2.8mi; 1h45min; grade, equipment, access as main walk. Start at the top gate (Rycroft) and follow the main walk until it reaches the centre of the figure-of-eight (56min). At this point, instead of turning left down the path towards Newlands Forest, keep walking along the jeep track, picking up the main walk again at the 2h25min-point. Note that nearly all of this version is exposed to the sun.

2   Newlands Forest. 5km/3mi; 2h. Grade and equipment as main walk. Access by 🚗: drive along Newlands Avenue towards Kirstenbosch and turn right at the traffic lights into Union Avenue (see Car tour 1 and *Street guide: Cape Town*). Park on the forest side of Union Avenue, in the lay-by near the junction. Climb up the embankment onto a pavement and walk uphill for about 300m/yds, then take a footpath turning left into the trees. After passing through a gap in a fence it continues to an open area next to a jeep track (11min). There is a walkers' map here, on the far side of the track. Turn left up the jeep track and zigzag past four forks off to the left. The fourth is a track (20min) coming in from Paradise Ruins: from this junction follow the main walk from the 1h08min-point. At the 2h-point in the main walk you rejoin the jeep track on which you set off: turn left here and return to Union Avenue by your outward route.

Note that there are a number of shorter walks in Kirstenbosch and Newlands Forest which you can plan from the maps in this book and from a number of poster maps erected in both areas. These walks are more easily planned from a map than a written description.

This walk explores Kirstenbosch Botanical Gardens and Newlands Forest, two of the Cape's best-known natural attractions. Between them they offer a wide variety of scenery ranging from dense woodland to open parkland. Lying on the eastern slopes of Table Mountain, the gardens and forest occupy large tracts of hilly territory that once formed part of Cecil Rhodes' estate. The gardens particularly are amongst the most beautiful in the world, laid out a few years after Rhodes' death on land bequeathed for the purpose in his will. Trees, shrubs and flowers from all over the world are grown here, attracting hosts of birds and insects to help with their continued survival. The gardens also feature in the cultural life of the city, with open-air concerts in summer and exhibitions covering a wide range of interests all year round.

From a walker's point of view this is intriguing country indeed. Both the gardens and the forest are criss-crossed by a maze of paths crying out for exploration. I suggest that you look over the large-scale map inside the back cover *before* you start out and keep the map handy as you walk, but the route is really quite straightforward.

To begin, go through the gates on the far side of Rhodes Drive and follow a tarred track, with the gardens sloping down to your right. The track rises steadily, its surface soon turning to brick paving. After about 600m/0.4mi it arrives at a major junction where the main track swings down to the right and another goes straight on. Take the latter; it rises steeply to a T-junction where you turn right (**11min**).

The track now changes to gravel and traverses north across the mountainside above the gardens — constantly rising and falling and providing occasional glimpses of the False Bay coastline and the long profile of mountains beyond: the Hottentots-Holland range to the left and the Kogelberge to the right. The track crosses three major streams over the next 20 minutes (Nursery, Skeleton and Window), before reaching a four-way junction (**33min**).

Turn right there, following the signs to Lubbert's Gift, Newlands Forest and the Yellow-wood Trail. The track descends the mountainside at first and then traverses left, before narrowing into a path and entering a wood. Soon the path turns left uphill (still signposted to Newlands Forest). Eventually the path levels out at yet another sign-post indicating you're on the right route (**48min**).

The path then changes to a jeep track once more. (*Shortly after the track starts, a path joins it from the Contour Path above on the left. This is the last of the descending paths to the gardens mentioned in Walk 1*). Your track descends steeply through woodland at first, then runs through open country until it reaches another path going off left to Newlands Forest (**56min**). This path, at the bottom of the hill, marks the centre of the figure-of-eight, a short section common to both the outward and return journeys. (*Short walk 1 returns to the gate from here.*) Follow the path down to the left, past a notice welcoming you at last to Newlands Forest. The path turns right beyond the notice and descends gradually through a small plantation of gum trees.

After walking through the trees for about 200m/yds, a vague path goes off obliquely to the left towards a short wooden pole bearing a pictogram of a match-stick jogger (**1h02min**). Turn left at the pole and follow a wide path over a stream and into a clearing, where the remnants of a number of early 18th-century stone buildings lie on both sides of the path — Paradise Ruins. The path ends at the far side of the ruins at an unmarked junction shaped like a hay-fork. Take the right prong (wide enough to qualify as a jeep track); follow it past another track going right, to another junction (**1h08min**), where you turn left up a wider jeep track. *(This is where the second loop of the figure-of-eight starts and where Short walk 2 joins the main walk.)* The track curls uphill steadily through mixed woodland for about 500m/0.3mi, before swinging sharply to the left at an easing of the gradient (**1h20min**).

Bear right at the bend, along a narrow path which soon forks among a scattering of rocks and roots: bear left here (the right-hand fork descends steeply out of sight). The path, such as it is, soon reaches a much broader path rising steadily to the left, high above a stream on the right. This path continues through mixed woodland, veers to the right over the stream and then traverses across the mountainside until it reaches another jeep track (**1h35min**).

Turn left and follow the track uphill for a few hundred metres/yards, until it rounds a hairpin bend to the left. At this point veer off to the right down a well-trodden path which swings sharply left and arrives soon afterwards at another good path at a skew-junction. Cut back right and follow this new path downhill through dense woodland on the right-hand side of yet another stream, which it crosses in due course, over an awkward jumble of boulders. The path continues downstream on the far bank, forking right halfway down, so as to stay near the stream. It then drops on to a broad jeep track by a small spreading tree with a bench underneath it (**1h50min**).

Turn right over a bridge across the stream and then left at a fork a few paces further on. Continue along the jeep track until it joins another coming in from the left about 600m/0.4mi past the fork (**2h**). *(Short walk 2 turns left here.)* Turn right here and follow the track uphill past three other forks going off to the left. Immediately after the third turn-off, veer left on a track, by another bench (**2h10min**). This soon leads you back to Paradise Ruins at the centre of the figure-of-eight. After crossing the stream, remember to turn right at the pole with the jogger, and walk through the gum trees and on to the path back to Kirstenbosch.

Keep left when the path reaches the jeep track (**2h 25min**). *(Short walk 1 continues from this point.)* The track runs downhill at first and then levels out, affording long views to the south — towards Constantiaberg on the right

Fernwood Buttress from near Rycroft Gate, where the walk starts and ends. This cliff rises 1000m/3300ft high on Table Mountain's eastern face.

and a ridge of mountains further down the peninsula to the left: Muizenberg and Lakeside Ridge. The track eventually arrives at a four-way junction where a signpost indicates that the gardens lie to the right. From now on just follow the signs to the gardens, keeping left when in doubt, until the gravelled track arrives at a garden fence made of wooden palings (on the left). Turn right opposite the fence, towards 'Smutspad', and go left at the next T-junction, just after the track crosses the Skeleton Gorge stream. This track then drops to another wide brick path on the edge of the cultivated section of the gardens (**2h50min**).

From here there are various ways of getting back to the gate, all of them short but not necessarily easy to find. The route described takes you through The Dell, a hidden garden of indigenous shrubs, trees and water-plants. Turn right when you reach the paved path and walk across a bridge over the Nursery Ravine stream, then past a herb garden and a stone sundial on the left, before turning right along a narrow cobbled path signposted to The Dell (next to an imposing red walnut tree). After a short distance leave the cobbled path as it veers right: continue straight ahead over a sloping lawn, to a wide cobbled path with a stone building beyond it (one of the few lavatories in the gardens). The heavily-shaded path bears left and enters The Dell, soon reaching Colonel Bird's Bath, which is filled with clear spring water and surrounded with tree-ferns — one of many species of indigenous plants that thrive in these warm and damp conditions. The area around this glen is a favourite haunt of fruit bats which live in caves further up the mountain. They come down to the gardens after dark and eat waterberries, wild figs and the fruit of the yellow-woods, dispersing the seed around the gardens.

Continue round the bath and then zigzag left uphill and out into the open through a throng of cycads — prehistoric shrubs standing around like a solemn gathering of prickly Humpty Dumpties. Keep climbing up the hillside by any one of a myriad of paths until you reach a *tarred* track at the top. Turn left here, back to Rycroft Gate (**3h05min**).

3 TABLE MOUNTAIN VIA CECILIA RAVINE AND RETURN VIA NURSERY RAVINE

See map inside back cover to begin; see also photograph pages 48-49

Distance/time: 9.5km/5.9mi; 3h

Grade: moderate to strenuous. Sure-footedness is a great help on the steep descent in Nursery Ravine, but there is little exposure. The ascent of Cecilia Ravine is tiring on a hot day. Climb 600m/1970ft.

Equipment: walking boots, sunhat, jersey, waterproofs, picnic, water; long-sleeved shirt and suncream in sunny weather

How to get there and return: 🚐 Follow Car tour 1 past *both* Kirstenbosch gates and continue along Rhodes Drive for a further 1.3km. There is an opening among the trees to the right which leads to a parking area, with more parking space on the other side of the road about 50 metres back.

Short walks

1 Cecilia Forest — waterfall — Kirstenbosch — Cecilia Forest. 4.5km/2.8mi; 1h35min. Moderate. Equipment and access as main walk. Follow the main walk to a point halfway up the third zigzag on the path up Spilhaus Ravine (42min) and continue straight ahead instead of climbing up to the left. After dipping down to a waterfall, the path continues undulating until it descends to the Contour Path above Kirstenbosch Gardens, by a large signpost (1h05min). Turn right here and follow the path back to the car park; it will join the outward path at the gum tree described in the main walk.

2 Cecilia Forest — Cecilia and Spilhaus ravines — Cecilia Forest. 3.5km/2.2mi; 1h20min. Moderate. Stout shoes will suffice. Access as main walk. Follow the main walk to the overgrown jeep track in Spilhaus Ravine, then turn down left as the track bends right (50min). Follow the path downhill into a pine plantation (where it negotiates a very long zigzag), then drop down onto a stony jeep track (1h05min). You can now see the Contour Path nearby on the right (it is still a jeep track at this point). Follow the Contour Path/jeep track to the left, until you arrive back at the gum tree junction, and walk back from there.

This walk is a good introduction to the Back Table of Table Mountain, which in many ways is more attractive than the high Front Table. It is less crowded, with no cable-car to provide easy access. It is also less bare and flat, with many streams and flowers to gladden the eye all the year round. And the views from the path towards False Bay and the rolling countryside to the distant eastern mountains are as good as you'll find anywhere — all this with the expenditure of relatively little effort. The route takes you from Cecilia Forest up to the Table's eastern escarpment and down again via a cleft further north called Nursery Ravine. From the bottom of the ravine, you follow the Contour Path back to Cecilia Forest. At its highest point, the ridge above Nursery Ravine, the path reaches an altitude of 750m/2460ft and at its lowest, in Cecilia Forest, 160m/525ft.

A special feature of this walk is the leisurely climb through the Cecilia and Spilhaus ravines, two of the most beautiful on the mountain. The two intertwine halfway down the mountainside, each as wild and colourful as the other. To see them at their best start early on an autumn or spring morning, when hanging gardens of green *fynbos* show off the subtle colours of the flowers in the early light. The mists that cling to the black poplars and pines at the foot of the ravines are special too — epitomising the atmosphere of the Cape countryside when it sleeps quietly beyond the reach of the summer sun.

To start out, go through the open gateway at the top right-hand corner of the car park, onto a jeep track (the larger-scale map inside the back cover can be used). After only a few paces leave the track and walk up the embankment on the right, through a pine plantation (no path, just worn earth). Keep uphill through the trees until a stepped path appears beyond a large weathered rock (about 300m/ yds from the gateway). Climb the path, then turn right onto another jeep track. Walk past a track coming in from the left and continue straight ahead. About 250m/yds further on the track crosses a stream (**12min**). Turn left here and follow a path skirting the left-hand bank of the stream.

The path rises through woodland for a few hundred metres/yards before crossing the main Contour Path at a three-way junction of jeep tracks (offset a little to the right). Note the large gum tree overlooking this junction. The path then continues rising through woodland until it reaches the end of yet another jeep track, where an old rectangular concrete water tank stands on the left (**22min**).

After crossing the track the path soon shakes off the trees and begins to zigzag up to the left of Cecilia Ravine and into Spilhaus Ravine. It is here that you begin to get your bearings, as a view of the distant scenery unfolds for the first time, growing ever wider as the path climbs higher. In the middle of the third and last zigzag (a very long one) a steep path climbs up to the left (**42min**). *(Short walk 1 goes straight on here.)* Follow the path to the left until it joins an

This waterfall in Spilhaus Ravine — a tributary of the Klaasenbosch — is in full flow after winter rain.

overgrown jeep track. The track continues the path's left-ward traverse across Spilhaus Ravine and then bends to the right as it enters a pine forest (**50min**). (*Short walk 2 branches off left here.*) After rising steadily for a few hundred metres/yards, the track begins a gentle descent; here you will see a path sloping up to the right through the trees (**54min**).

Climb this path for a short distance, up to a jeep track paved with concrete, where you turn right. When the track swings sharply left (by a scattering of rocks on the right) a fine view of Table Mountain's eastern escarpment can be seen. The track then zigzags up to the head of Spilhaus Ravine, crossing the stream at its centre over a bridge lying some distance above the tree line. (Make sure you keep right at the hairpin bend halfway up; the track going off left is a cul-de-sac). The track levels out beyond the bridge and slowly meanders across the top of the escarpment, revealing a huge arc of distant horizons and a wide expanse of semi-camouflaged suburbia at the mountain's eastern feet.

There is a strategically placed water tap outside a stone cottage on the right-hand side of the track after it has cleared Cecilia Ravine (though the water is often heavily chlorinated). Shortly afterwards, as the track bends left, a broad path continues straight ahead (**1h30min**). Leave the track and follow the path as it meanders picturesquely through a mixture of thick *fynbos* and rock for about 1km/0.6mi. Much of the distant horizon vanishes at this point, beyond the boundaries of this intimate garden. Halfway across, the path comes to a stone wall overlooking a brown pond swimming with weeds, tadpoles and frogs. It then ambles up the other side and on towards a narrow ravine where it swings left and begins a short climb.

Take the *third* path to the right after the path has finished climbing and cross a stream via a small wooden bridge. The path then climbs over a low ridge and descends to the top of the next gorge: Nursery Ravine (**1h55min**). Now a bird's-eye view of the reservoir at Kirstenbosch suddenly appears, lying some 500m/1640ft below. The rest of the gardens are hidden by Nursery Buttress (photograph pages 48-49) to the left, but a short walk to the front of Castle Rocks at the top of the buttress will widen the prospect considerably. The view down the ravine from the saddle is made all the more dramatic by the vertical rock wall of Nursery Buttress plunging dizzily down to the left, opposite a descending staircase of craggy stone ramparts tumbling down to the right. The derelict tree nursery that lends its name to the ravine is some distance behind you.

For the next 30 minutes or so you will need to keep your wits about you, for the ravine is very steep and rocky, particularly at the outset. Keep a look-out for black eagles which sometimes perch on the rocks to the right, or more likely swing across the ravine below you looking for prey. The descent ends at the Contour Path, where you turn right and cross a jumble of heavy boulders in the Nursery stream (**2h**). Shortly afterwards, after bending sharply to the left at the next stream, the path forks. Go right (signposted to Constantianek) and continue until you reach the three-way junction of jeep tracks met on the outward journey.

This time, however, instead of taking the downhill path back to the car park, fork left at the junction and carry on along the lower jeep track for about 400m/yds, until you reach a closed gate. Take the path in front of the gate, dropping downhill to the left. When you reach the jeep track you followed near the start of the walk, head down to the car park through the pine trees (**3h**).

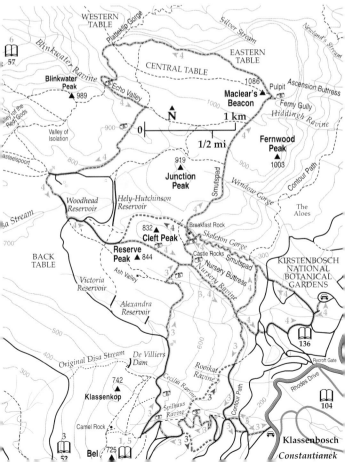

4 THE SUMMIT OF TABLE MOUNTAIN FROM THE BOTANICAL GARDENS AT KIRSTENBOSCH

Map page 45, but see also larger-scale map inside the back cover

Distance/time: 15km/9.3mi; 6h

Grade: strenuous — a long walk with many rocky climbs and descents. *Take care after rain,* especially about halfway up Skeleton Gorge, where the stream runs down the path, and on the descent in Nursery Ravine; both sections are hazardous when wet. Climb 1050m/3450ft.

Equipment: walking boots, sunhat, jersey, waterproofs, picnic, plenty of water; suncream and long-sleeved shirt in sunny weather

How to get there and return: 🚗 Enter Kirstenbosch by the bottom gate and park in the car park at the end of the access drive (see Car tour 1, page 11, and the *Street guide: Cape Town*).

Short walks: Several interesting walks can be enjoyed on the Top Table by taking the cable car to the summit. Well-marked trails lasting from 30min to 1h30min provide remarkable views without effort. Grades are easy, and normal walking clothes and shoes are adequate. There is a restaurant next to the upper cable station.

Alternative walk: Skeleton Gorge — Hely-Hutchinson Reservoir — Nursery Ravine. 8km/5mi; 3h30min. Equipment, grade and access as main walk (climb 700m/2300ft). Follow the main walk to the top of Skeleton Gorge (1h30min) and then keep straight on instead of turning right. Soon after passing a sign pointing to Kasteelspoort, the path becomes very sandy and begins to skirt the boundary fence along the southern shore of the Hely-Hutchinson Reservoir. After a few hundred metres the fence bends sharply to the right (near an old signless post). Your path goes straight on, away from the reservoir, and rejoins the main walk very soon afterwards (at a signpost pointing left to Nursery Ravine). Return to the gardens from here, following the main walk from the 4h45min point.

This is one of the classic walks of the Cape: Jan Smuts' route to the summit of Table Mountain — a pilgrimage for anyone with a sense of history. People have been climbing this mountain for many years, particularly in the recent past, as more and more routes have been opened. But for Jan Smuts — lawyer, soldier, statesman and philosopher — *this* was the way to the top: a route that he followed almost until his death in 1950 at the age of 80. His path is a simple one: it climbs the eastern flank of the mountain and then goes north along its eastern escarpment to the topmost point — Maclear's Beacon. The walk described here extends his route along the mountain's northern escarpment and then across some of its central valleys and ridges before returning by a different ravine.

The extension not only adds some variety to the walk, but it also creates an opportunity to appreciate the mountain's special atmosphere — its hidden valleys and peaks, its weathered rocks and tiny streams, and the fragrance and beauty of its abundant flora. The remarkable thing is that although that flora is under constant threat from encroachment and erosion, the mountain still boasts some 1400

46

different species of indigenous plant, a significant propor-
tion of the Cape floral kingdom's total population of 8600
species. Not everything is in flower at the same time
obviously, but even in winter there is plenty to look at and
admire — particularly for someone with a practised eye.

The hike starts from the car park at the upper end of the
main entrance from Rhodes Avenue — the bottom gate.
Walk through a turnstile to the left (for a nominal fee) and
then between some strategetically-positioned shops. Cross a
broad stone pavement and descend two flights of steps to
a paved track leading to the right. Follow it across a wooden
bridge over a stream, then turn right on a gravel jeep track
leading upwards towards the mountain (signposted to
Skeleton Gorge and Smutspad). The stream you have just
crossed is the Skeleton Gorge stream, one of three forming
the Liesbeek River below Rhodes Avenue. The track
follows the stream. A few hundred metres/yards further on,
after the track bends sharply to the left, take a narrow path
off to the right signposted to Skeleton Gorge. Both track and
path lead to the gorge, but the path follows a dark and
intriguing route through dense woodland. They rejoin just
before reaching a jeep track running across the mountain.
In late spring and early summer — October and November
— this wood echoes to the call of the red-chested cuckoo.*

Carry on across the track and climb a well-worn and
stepped path on the far side, again signposted to Skeleton
Gorge; the stream is still on your right as the path makes its
way up to the Contour Path (**30min**). There is a sign on a
rock on the far side of the Contour Path which confirms
you're still following 'Smutspad'. This gorge is the steepest
part of the climb, some 400m/1300ft high. There are
ladders and chains fixed to the rock to help you over a
tricky section about halfway up, after which the path
follows the boulder-strewn streambed for a short distance.
Apart from that section the way is straightforward, eventually climbing to a narrow saddle at the summit of the
gorge. Only when the path crosses the stream on the last
section of the climb does it emerge from dense woodland

*Slightly smaller than its European cousin and with a more pronounced
red collar, it is known in Afrikaans as a *Piet-my-vrou* (Pete-my-wife). This
mystifying phrase has its origins in early Afrikaans folklore, when people
led isolated lives and justice was sometimes slow and rough. The story
goes that Piet killed his mistress's husband so as to obtain uninterrupted
possession. The husband's despairing spirit took over the cuckoo's and
flew from tree to tree asking Piet where his wife was. Sometimes three
notes are called and sometimes four: 'Piet, waar's my vrou?'; the first note
high and shrill, the next two or three still loud but in descending harmony.

into a mixture of small trees and *fynbos*. The path reaches a junction (**1h30min**) as it approaches the saddle through a thicket of trees. *(The Alternative walk goes straight ahead here.)* The path to the left leaves the trees and goes up to Breakfast Rock. It was in the shade of this large rock that Jan Smuts was reputed to have had his breakfast on his way to the top — his second breakfast probably!

Our path to the summit of Table Mountain goes off right at this junction and soon starts to climb out of the gorge. The way is steep at first, but after about 100m/300ft of ascent the path levels out and makes for the next ravine: Window Gorge. At the height of summer, from late January to March, red disas flower on the banks of the stream running down towards that gorge, both upstream and downstream of the wooden bridge that crosses it. In fact, if one is lucky enough to find a cool day and starts walking early, that time of the year is the best to tackle this walk.

Smutspad continues its steady northeasterly climb from Window Gorge, crossing several thick layers of rock on the way and passing two paths coming in from the left. For the most part the way is obvious, but there is a tricky bit beyond a group of huge free-standing rocks perched on each side of the path (the one to the right shaped like a blacksmith's anvil): beyond these tall rocks the path travels over bedrock, twisting right and left before passing another plaque with Smuts' name on it, pinned to a rock on the left.

Just before the path climbs some wooden steps on its last lap towards Maclear's Beacon, another path goes off right over a series of flat rocks: take it; it's worth investigating. It soon arrives at a rocky platform overlooking the eastern edge of the mountain (beneath the Top Table). A labyrinth of deep rocky gorges and buttresses lies below, including Ascension Ravine, Ferny Gully and the Pulpit — the latter a huge rock stump whose ecclesiastical bulk rises stolidly some 900m/2950ft above sea level between the two precipitous gorges. Several pines decorate the Pulpit's rugged profile, in various states of penury.

Smutspad misses all this drama out, of course, very soon climbing to the top at Maclear's Beacon, 1086m/3560ft high and only 5.5km from Kirstenbosch; it invariably seems a lot more, since it takes a good **2h30min** to get here. The beacon, which appears very suddenly, consists of a huge pile of stones shaped like an igloo or beehive and commemorates the survey point established here in 1844 by Sir Thomas Maclear, an Irish astronomer and surveyor.

From this point one gets a very good idea of the enormous size of the mountain's summit, spreading out in all directions in a series of shallow bogs and rock debris strewn about on the flat sandstone. The beacon is high up on an extensive natural pedestal of solid rock that overlooks the rest of the table. The view to distant horizons is rivalled only by the view from the summit of Devil's Peak.

In fact, the latter forms the only impediment to a 360-degree panorama which takes in ocean, bay, peninsula, hinterland and the Atlantic shoreline heading north into the dim distance.

As the path clambers down the northern side of the pedestal near the beacon, a memorial to Smuts, in the form of another plaque, can be seen pinned to the rock. It reads 'His life was gentle; and the elements / So mixed in him that Nature might stand up / And say to all the world "This was a man!".' The quotation is, of course, Mark Antony's tribute to Brutus, delivered in the

Nursery Buttress — one of the Back Table's major landmarks. Nursery Ravine is to the left of the buttress. (Car tour 1, Picnic 2)

A ridge of weathered rock leading to Reserve Peak

dying moments of Shakespeare's *Julius Caesar.* Nevertheless, the tribute sits well on Smuts' austere shoulders.

From Smuts' plaque the path continues in a northwesterly direction across the width of the Front Table, sometimes on flat rock, sometimes across wooden pathways raised above boggy soil. After about 0.5km/0.3mi the path emerges on the front face of the table and meanders along the top, fairly close to the edge. Fortunately the northeastern face of the mountain is not sheer where the path follows it, so you can concentrate on the scenery in relative comfort — the northern coastline rolling away into the distance and the rambling city below. This is also an area where black eagles hunt their favoured prey: dassies (rock-rabbits), little creatures the size of rabbits. Their tiny droppings can be seen heaped on shaded rocks.

About 1km/0.6mi from the beacon the path leaves the edge and makes its way inland, following the line of a huge gully that splits the face of the mountain at an angle, moving eastwards as it descends. This gully, Platteklip Gorge, was the route the early settlers took to the top from the garrison below. In fact, it is reported to have been climbed as early as 1503 by Portuguese sailors on their way round the Cape, led by a gentleman called Antonio de Saldanha. The path soon descends to the top of this gorge, from where a network of other paths branches out. A three-way signpost marks this four-way crossroad (**3h15min**) our path is the unmarked one going southwards — in the opposite direction to Platteklip Gorge. The path soon leads downhill to one of the fingers of Blinkwater Ravine (North Gully), whereupon it turns left and begins to circumnavigate the ravine — another very large gully, but facing west this time. The route is circuitous and tricky at times as it drops down several small rock faces covered by steep ladders bolted into the rock.

The path descends to Echo Valley at the head of Blinkwater Ravine, from where a view of the Atlantic is framed by the rocky sides of the ravine. Take the path that branches off left soon afterwards and walk southeast along the floor of the valley — back towards Maclear's Beacon. About 0.5km/0.3mi along you come to a crossroad, where a small wooden bridge carries a path over the stream to the left. Take the opposite path, going uphill to the right and climbing about 50m/150ft, to another crest (**4h**). A view of the Hely-Hutchinson and Woodhead reservoirs opens out from this ridge, the latter to the right, downstream of the former. The Hely-Hutchinson Reservoir (built in 1904) was named after the then governor of the Cape, and the Woodhead (built in 1897) after the man who was Cape Town's mayor at the time. All those years ago, before the reservoirs flooded them out, hosts of red disas used to grow on the banks of the stream running down that valley.

From the top of the rise above the valley, the path runs diagonally downhill to the right across the flanks of both reservoirs. On passing some forestry buildings, you join a concrete road and follow it to a clearing, where the road curves to the right. Here take the path off to the left, opposite a water tap (another three-way signpost at a four-way crossroad). You descend to the Woodhead Reservoir wall, a massive structure, beautifully made with carefully-dressed stones. The path (guarded by an iron railing) runs along the top of the wall, with the curved and weathered face plunging down to the river below in a spectacular concave drop.

Once the path reaches the far end of the dam wall it climbs to another forestry road paved with concrete. Follow this road to the left until it reaches a rough but clear jeep track going off right — about 300m/yds from the wall. Follow the track uphill until it veers left and narrows into a path, heading for the Hely-Hutchinson Reservoir. Here take a wide path off to the right (signposted 'Nursery Ravine'; **4h45min**). *(The Alternative walk rejoins here.)* You climb above the Hely-Hutchinson Reservoir towards a brow between two hills — Reserve Peak to the right and Cleft Peak to the left. When the path reaches the brow a few hundred metres/yards beyond the signpost, long views across oceans of water to the west and mountainous country to the east open out. In the eastern foreground is the nursery after which the ravine was named; its remains contain many varieties of alien trees, including oaks, pines, cedars and birches. Steep rock-strewn slopes rise on either side of the narrow valley, sheltering the nursery from wind and driving rain. The soft fertile soil along the way is covered with protective wooden walkways, until the path veers a little to the right, rising above the floor of the nursery and into rocky country once more.

Soon afterwards the path reaches the end of the valley and turns left at another signpost where it descends to the head of Nursery Ravine — 12km from the starting point and about 1km to the south of Skeleton Gorge (**5h**). To all intents and purposes the path has completed a ragged rectangle. Far below, at the bottom of the ravine, lies a small reservoir which provides water for the gardens. The Nursery Ravine descent, of about 400m/1300ft, is divided into three natural sections: a rocky section at the top (quite short but tricky), an open zigzag stretch brightened by many wild flowers (king proteas among them), and then a long section in dense woodland close to the stream. The stream flows down the ravine at the right of the path in a series of steep pitches and waterfalls. After rain the sound of falling water is constant as it dashes down in a straight line, widening out at each cliff face before pouring over the boulders strewn across the Contour Path and tumbling down the mountainside into the gardens below.

On reaching the Contour Path, you may wish to refer again to the larger-scale map inside the back cover. Turn right across the stream and walk under heavy shade for a few hundred metres/ yards, then fork left on an open path. It descends to a wide gravel track. Turn left again, through a mixture of open *fynbos* and silver trees. Then go right about 100m/yds further on. This downhill path leads to another gravel track, where you again turn left. Very soon, take a wide paved track that descends steeply to the right, into the cultivated section of the gardens. Fork left at the bottom of the steep section and follow the curving track downhill until it descends two flights of stone steps. From there any number of paths lead back to the car park (**6h**).

Camel Rock — a landmark on Walk 5

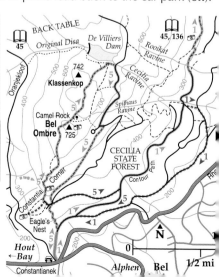

5 CONSTANTIA CORNER

See map and photograph opposite

Distance 6km/3.7mi; 2h45min

Grade: strenuous during the initial climb to the summit of Bel Ombre; the rest of the walk is easy. Take care when climbing the face of the peak, as the path is loose in places. There is some scrambling near the top. Climb 550m/1800ft.

Equipment: walking boots are preferable, otherwise stout shoes, jersey, waterproofs, sunhat, picnic, plenty of water; suncream and long-sleeved shirt in sunny weather

How to get there and return: 🚌 Follow Car tour 1 (page 11) as far as Constantianek and park in the open area to the north of the roundabout — on the opposite side from the restaurant.

Short walk: Eagle's Nest from Constantianek. 1km/0.6mi; 1h. Grade, equipment, access as main walk. Climb 207m/680ft. Follow the main walk up to the saddle between Eagle's Nest and Constantia Corner. The summit of Eagle's Nest is about a 10min climb from here, up to the left: there are several paths, all of which come together on the top. It is a very good viewing point indeed, just as good as any higher up. On the way down you can avoid the steep descent through the pine trees by taking the jeep track instead (keep right at the junction further down). It should take about 30min to return by the jeep track, less by the path.

This is a relatively short walk, half in shade and half out: a mixture of mountainside and forest. It's one of the quickest ways to the top of the Back Table, and by virtue of its position at the southern end of the mountain, it is a particularly good vantage point. Take the map *Approved paths on Table Mountain* with you (see page 4): you'll be able to pick out nearly all the peaks on the Back Table, as well as many to the south further down the peninsula.

This walk owes its title to Table Mountain's shape — a rough rectangle with four corners. Three have the name 'Corner' attached to them: Kloofnek to the northwest, Hout Bay to the southwest and Constantia to the southeast. (The northeastern corner adjoins Devil's Peak). Of the three named, Constantia Corner is the only one qualifying as a 'walk'; the others require ropes. The prospects from all three corners are very fine indeed, this one no less than the others. In fact, the view is remarkable all the way up, a good reason for frequent pauses on this extremely steep climb. You can see a series of deep wooded valleys sloping down on either side of the *nek,* with Oranjekloof and Hout Bay nestling between the mountains to the west and a wider panorama to the south and east. The highest point of the climb, lying well back from the face, is called Bel Ombre — well-named, since its moving shadow is present all day. The path is shaded in the morning.

Start out from where you parked by walking up the tarred drive to the right. Go through the gate at the top and into Cecilia Forest, where the road becomes a jeep track. Then take a path to the left about 40m/yds beyond the gate; it climbs steeply through the trees to a junction of jeep tracks high above the gate (**20min**). Take the level track going left and then climb up to the right at a turning circle about 200m/yds from the junction. There are several paths, all of them leading to the saddle between Eagle's Nest to the left and Constantia Corner to the right.

Bear right at the saddle *(but for the Short walk climb up to the left)* and follow an obvious path which climbs steeply for a while before traversing left under a buttress, soon reaching a cairn where another path ascends to the right (**38min**). Climb up this path, which begins the ascent of the main face of Constantia Corner. After meandering to the right and returning to the centre of the rock face, the path forks (about 10 minutes beyond the cairn). Keep right and stay on the right of the rock face until the gradient eases beyond the first of two false horizons. (Note that the path going left at the fork should not be used: it is badly eroded.)

As the path works its way to the right before taking its first rest, the views to the east are truly impressive: forests in the foreground, the Cape flats and the bay in the middle distance, and range upon range of mountains on the horizon. One of the impressive things about this route is the speed with which one rises above the surrounding country-side! The path now meanders on until it reaches a rock face, where you will have an easy scramble to the top. Once you reach the top of the cliff, Bel Ombre's summit beacon heaves into sight for the first time; the false horizons are behind you now. But before climbing to the summit you *do* have to pass over another outcrop of rock with a very low overhang (duck!). (Note that when the path reaches this outcrop it *appears* to run along the foot of it to the left, but if you look carefully there is a way *over* the rock: the path swings up to the left before squeezing through a gap under the low overhang.)

The route across the summit is marked by cairns about 50m/yds to the left of the beacon (**1h25min**), which stands some 725m/2380ft above sea level. From here you have an interesting view of the Twelve Apostles on the western horizon — twelve high buttresses or peaks, starting from Porcupine Buttress to the north and finishing, appropriately, with Judas Peak to the south — the latter standing at the summit of Hout Bay Corner. You can see Judas Peak as a shallow pyramid a couple of peaks to the left of the high peak in front of you — 'Grootkop' (literally 'Big Head', out more usually translated as 'Great Peak'). Curiously enough, Judas is the only apostle mentioned by name.

The path continues down the rock on the far side, well to the left of the beacon, diving down into a labyrinth of large weathered rocks sunk deep in thick undergrowth. The path splits into three at this point, but all three routes manage to find their way through or round the deep clefts in the rock and descend to a narrow valley down to the left. Two of them pass a cave, a useful shelter in a rain squall.

As you cross the floor of the valley you'll get a worm's-eye view of a curious feature of this walk: a stone configuration on top of the next ridge which looks remarkably like a camel whose humps have worn down through old age. Camel Rock, it's called — a much-photographed icon of Table Mountain (see page 52). The path passes nonchalantly behind the camel's rear legs and then straight on over a much smaller ridge. (Note that the path really *does* cross the second ridge, despite appearances to the contrary. The broad path going right just in front of it peters out after only a hundred paces or so.)

Having found the path on the far side of the ridge, stick to it through thick and thin as it traverses the Back Table on a more or less level course until it dips down to a wide stretch of water called De Villiers Dam. Throughout this section the outline of the mountain's Front Table is clearly visible (given fine weather), with Maclear's Beacon on the right and the cable station on the left. Take the right fork as the path splits on its way down to the water, and walk out onto the concrete jeep track over to the right (**1h55min**).

The rest of the journey is easy. Turn right and follow the track as it circumnavigates the wide summits of the Cecilia and Spilhaus ravines before descending to a pine plantation. After skirting the trees for a short while, the track describes a hairpin bend to the left, past a gravel spur. Keep to the main track until you can take a path off to the right, about 200m/yds below the bend (**2h08min**). This wide, well-trodden path descends steadily in a southerly direction, the pine plantation still dropping down to the left, and the eastern flank of Bel Ombre rising abruptly to the right. It takes about 22 minutes to walk down this path before it reaches the jeep track again — just as the track approaches another hairpin bend. A gravel track goes off at a tangent here — the one leading to Eagle's Nest and Constantia Corner which you used briefly on the way up. Find your way down the steep path from here; it's a 15 minute descent back to the *nek* (**2h45min**).

6 THE DIAGONAL ROUTE TO THE AQUEDUCT AND RETURN VIA KASTEELSPOORT

Distance/time: 12km/7.4mi; 4h50min

Grade: strenuous, with some stiff climbs and descents and a small amount of scrambling. However, as the climb takes place on the western face of Table Mountain, the sun does not reach the ascending path until mid-morning — a bonus on a summer's day. Climb 700m/2300ft.

Equipment: walking boots, sunhat, jersey, waterproofs, picnic, water; long-sleeved shirt and suncream in sunny weather. Note that there is usually plenty of water in the Disa Stream on top of the mountain.

How to get there and return: 🚗 Take the road over Kloofnek described in Car tour 2 on pages 15-16 and turn left up Fiskaal Road 2.5km beyond Kloofnek. This road snakes up the mountainside, changing its name as it rises to Francolin and then Theresa. About 2.5km from the junction the road reaches its summit; park in the short cul-de-sac on the left, opposite 26 Theresa Avenue. The walk starts from the top of the cul-de-sac.

Alternative walk: Valley of the Red Gods — Kasteelspoort. 7km/4.3mi; 3h. Grade, equipment, access as main walk. Climb 600m/1970ft. Follow the main walk to the 2h-point, then descend directly to Kasteelspoort. Pick up the main walk again at the 4h-point.

This is one of the finest walks on Table Mountain: a kaleidoscope of colour and history. It differs from most walks in this book in that it crosses the face of the mountain diagonally as it climbs, grappling with three buttresses and three ravines on its way — instead of the usual one. It also explores the upper reaches of the Disa Gorge and the shores of two reservoirs before returning via Kasteelspoort (Castle Gate). Add a short rest in the Valley of the Red Gods and a visit to the mountain's museum, and you have the makings of a memorable trip. The walk is best undertaken in February when the disas are out in abundance (the drier the season, the earlier the flowers bloom).

Begin the walk by going round the gate at the top of the cul-de-sac and ascending the concrete jeep track on the far side. The track forks a few hundred metres/yards later (after passing a less obvious junction earlier on). Turn left here, following the new track until it reaches its summit — soon after changing from concrete to gravel. Now turn right on a narrow path and climb to a broad contour path: the Pipe Track. Turn left on the Pipe Track and follow it northwards until you come to a signpost pointing back to Kasteelspoort. Climb the unmarked path up to the right, on the far side of the post (**20min**). When you reach a band of rock with a cairn on top of it (**50min**), climb the rock and veer right. (Note that the path going right at the

56

bottom of the rock leads to an alarming dead end, while the path going left at the top leads to Blind Gully which is not recommended either.)

The path now wanders along a wide ledge across Porcupine Buttress before starting to ascend the gorge beyond it: Porcupine Ravine. After climbing for about 20 minutes you reach a large 'semi-detached' cairn — its back leaning against the rock (**1h15min**). This landmark is a godsend to those of us without a sense of direction, for this is a critical juncture in the climb. Fork right at this cairn: the stronger path going left carries on up the ravine, but your target is a wide ledge further up to the *right*. Once found, the path becomes increasingly obvious, winding its way confidently up to the ledge, where it continues to the right.

The ledge is a long one, crossing Jubilee Buttress, Jubilee Ravine and Barrier Buttress, before reaching Barrier Ravine — the route to the top. The views as you wend your way across the ledge, some 700m/2300ft above the sea, are worth lingering over. There's a particularly fine view of Lion's Head behind you, with Kloof Buttress rising to its right, leading up to the western edge of the Front Table, with the cable station at the top. The ledge narrows a bit as it crosses Jubilee Ravine, but there is little exposure. The climb to the top of Barrier Ravine is short (**1h50min**).

The path now descends into the Valley of the Red Gods, a quiet hollow overlooked by an arc of rocky figures silhouetted against the northern and eastern skylines. A stream flows down from the left, into a marsh of dark soil and thick protea. A scattering of red flowers lights the rising valley beyond, in vivid contrast to the surrounding rock and greenery. It is a picture of rare charm. While the valley is high enough and isolated enough for pagan gods to have

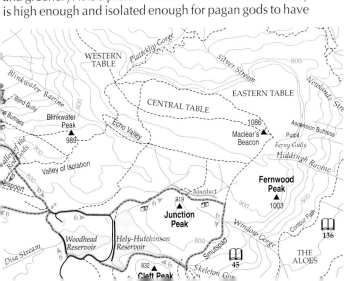

While a host of other flowers decorate this walk, it is the disas that really catch the eye. The ones you see by the stream and in the aqueduct further up are red disas — varieties of ground orchids. The flowers are pollinated by a large brown and orange butterfly called 'Mountain Pride', its wings marked with blue spots near the tips. The insect has a sort of Spanish-bull syndrome, being attracted by bright colours — red in particular.

gathered there long ago, a more plausible explanation for its name is that it was called after the last line of the refrain of Rudyard Kipling's poem *The feet of the young men.*

After crossing the stream the path reaches a broader path coming down from the left. Turn right here and descend through a narrow neck towards a wide plateau — the northern reaches of the Back Table. There are cottages to the left overlooking two large reservoirs, and a huge gorge dropping down to the right, its entrance bordered by vertical cliffs. This is Kasteelspoort (Castle Gate), your life-line back to the car and one of the most frequently-trodden gorges on the mountain. But there is more exploring to be done before tackling the gorge. Take a path going off left part-way down to the plateau (**2h**). *(But for the Alternative walk, keep straight ahead.)* Follow the path down to a jeep track which leads to the houses. Walk past a copse and a signpost and continue along the now-concreted jeep track, passing between a wire fence on the left and houses and workshops on the right. You reach the arched wall of the Hely-Hutchinson Reservoir, rising above a stone cottage (the museum mentioned earlier; it houses a display of equipment and plant used to build the reservoirs).

The path goes up to the left from the museum and then runs above the northern shore of Hely-Hutchinson until it reaches a stream. You're now approaching the upper reaches of the Disa Gorge — narrow, high and rugged, the water running down its centre the colour of burnished copper. The path keeps to the left of the stream at first, then crosses it via a concrete beam and begins climbing steeply up to a fine vantage point, before ambling steadily upwards alongside the stream. The disas can be seen almost as soon as the path closes in on the stream: lovely red flowers with three large petals, the upper one finely veined in white. Vivid red crassulas and pale *Watsonias* (members of the iris family) can also be found along the banks of the stream all the way up to the stone aqueduct at the top of the gorge (**2h45min**). The path crosses a railway-sleeper bridge over the aqueduct and then wanders along its southern wall. This channel is even more richly endowed with disas than

Lion's Head, seen from Porcupine Ravine on a lovely winter's morning

Disa Gorge. The aqueduct was built at the same time as the reservoirs, to divert the water from the Disa down to the dam. A solid structure, it mounts several steps halfway along and commands a fine view of the valley above Window Gorge below to the right and longer views over the eastern escarpment to the mountains beyond.

The path leaves the aqueduct at its eastern end and continues on a level course until it reaches the main path to Maclear's Beacon from Skeleton Gorge, at a point where it crosses an outcrop of rock. Your path descends the rock obliquely to the right and then runs down to the Window Gorge stream — another disa habitat. (Note that the path down the outcrop may be difficult to find. It hugs the right-hand edge like a flight of steps, only a few paces from where you emerge from the aqueduct path.)

Cross the stream on a wooden bridge and then follow the path down to the top of Skeleton Gorge, where a signpost points to Kasteelspoort. Take this path and head due west. You soon arrive at the Hely-Hutchinson Reservoir again and meander past the southern shores of both dams, before crossing the Woodhead Reservoir wall. Once you've climbed up the far side of the wall, take the path going left; it follows the track of the old railway line from Kasteelspoort. Follow it to its terminus, where you'll see the remains of the winch used to bring up building materials for the reservoirs. The remains stand on a wide platform of rock high above Kasteelspoort (**3h55min**).

Now rejoin the path you crossed shortly before arriving at the winch and descend to the ravine, a cavernous gorge penetrating deep into the mountain, overhung by precipitous cliffs on both sides. Turn left at the top of the ravine (signposted; **4h**). *(The Alternative walk rejoins here.)* Halfway down the ravine, below a platform of rock, the path veers right and descends to the Pipe Track at a point close to where you joined it on the way up. Cross the track and descend a rough path on the far side; it soon joins the concrete jeep track coming up from Theresa Avenue. Walk down to the gate (**4h50min**), keeping left at both junctions on the way down.

7 MYBURGH WATERFALL RAVINE, JUDAS PEAK AND LLANDUDNO RAVINE

Distance/time: 11km/6.8mi; 4h45min

Grade: strenuous. The route is often steep, with plenty of scrambling on the way up and some on the way down. The path is good most of the time, but eroded and strewn with loose rock in several sections of the descent down Llandudno Ravine. The path up Myburgh Waterfall Ravine, somewhat vague at the outset, ceases to exist halfway up — where the ravine is choked with fallen rock. *Note that this walk is strictly for summer; it becomes dangerous when the rains begin in April or May.* Climb 600m/1970ft.

Equipment: walking boots, sunhat, jersey, waterproofs, picnic, water; long-sleeved shirt and suncream in sunny weather

How to get there and return: 🚗 Follow Car tour 2 (page 16) all the way past Llandudno, to the turning to Suikerbossie, where you turn left. Then take the next turning left — again signposted to Suikerbossie (Sugar Bush). Park at the top of the rise just above the main road (note the plaque on the left dedicated to Thomas Bain, the Scottish engineer).

Short walk: Little Lion's Head. 2.5km/1.6mi; 1h30min. Strenuous: very steep all the way, with some tricky scrambling at the top. Climb 280m/ 920ft. Equipment and access as main walk. From your parking place, clamber down the embankment, cross the main road, and then walk up the road to the right — until the terrain levels out on the left. This is where the path up the mountain begins; it is overgrown at first, but clears as it passes a TV relay station about a quarter of the way up. Near the summit, the scrambling can be reduced by keeping right at a cairn standing on top of a rock above you, instead of making for the neighbouring cairn to the left. Descend the same way and, to avoid getting lost in the thick under-growth near the bottom, keep to the line of telegraph poles once the path reaches it.

Alternative walk: Myburgh Waterfall Ravine. 7km/4.3mi; 2h30min. Moderate. Equipment and access as main walk. Follow the main walk to the first waterfall — an ideal picnic spot when in full spate. Then return to the upper contour path, descend Myburgh Waterfall Ravine to the lower contour path and follow it back to the junction above Hout Bay Corner. From here retrace steps back to your car.

This is one of the most picturesque routes on Table Mountain, a circular walk on its southernmost slopes. There are glorious views all the way round, and a cool and beautiful ravine to climb at the outset. The best time to walk here is in February or March, when the disas are out. There are some fine specimens of both the red (*Uniflora*) and the blue (*Herschelianthe graminifolia*) varieties in Myburgh Waterfall Ravine. The ascent is steep but full of interest, at first running through indigenous wood-land, then squeezing between high cliffs,

From the summit of Judas Peak — Hout Bay, with Chapman's Peak in the distance

finally out in the open, in thick *fynbos*. There are two waterfalls en route (both dry in summer) — the first in dark woodland and the second open to the sky.

To begin the walk take the broad footpath opposite Bain's plaque (waymarked to the Back Table). Then turn left at the first junction (also waymarked). Walk uphill alongside the perimeter fence of Suikerbossie Restaurant and join another path coming in from the right. Keep going steadily uphill to the left until the path bends to the right and forks three ways. Take the right-hand fork and keep straight on through two junctions, to a double column of pine trees (**15min**). The lower contour path goes straight on here, but your path turns left through the pines and then goes right on the upper contour path 50m/yds further up.

Now follow the upper contour path to the right across the mountain, passing another double row of pine trees and two gorges, before reaching wooded Myburgh Waterfall Ravine (**1h20min**). The contour path begins to lose altitude now, but take another path to the left here, rising through the trees, with the stream down to your right. The path keeps to the left of the stream, which is out of sight among trees. Ignore any paths going left or right on this section — they either rejoin the main path or disappear into the stream. After **1h35min** the path arrives at what appears to be a dead-end — an arched cliff at the centre of the stream: the first waterfall.

Cut back to the left once you've reached the waterfall — it isn't a dead-end after all. Climb the path *behind* you, gently at first and then more steeply as you rise straight up the left bank of the stream and into open terrain. Here the

path levels out, re-enters the trees and resumes its steady upward journey alongside the stream. Shortly afterwards it joins the streambed again and follows a series of cairns to a vantage point below another cliff at the right of the stream (**1h45min**). With luck you should get your first sighting of red disas here (see photograph page 58). Your path now follows the steep narrow gorge up to the left, clambering over an avalanche of fallen boulders. After about 25 minutes of climbing up the rock, the path — such as it is — reaches the second waterfall; you're out of the woods at last (**2h10min**). This time you have to climb the waterfall — via a series of rock ledges, with small clusters of red disas clinging to the wet soil at the side. Take care here; the rock is sometimes slippery, even in summer.

At the top of the waterfall take the path leading abruptly left; it then swings right on an easy uphill gradient to the top of the ravine. It's worth pausing on the way up to take in the view to the east, framed by the sloping sides of the ravine. Below is the wooded valley leading from Constantianek down to Hout Bay. Beyond it to the right are Vlakkenberg and Constantiaberg, while straight ahead is Constantia Corner, with the Eagle's Nest at its feet and Bel Ombre silhouetted at the right of the high ridge at the top.

From now on the way is easy to find. Keep following the path as it winds its overgrown way through a wide valley thickly populated with heather and *Leucadendrum* (a variety of protea). After reaching the end of the valley, the path arrives at a large cairn with a smaller one to its left. This is where the path from the ravine ends, at a meeting point with the path running along the top of Table Mountain's western escarpment (**2h45min**). A little to the right is the southern face of Separation Buttress. The beacon on the peak to your left marks the summit of the twelfth apostle: Judas Peak. This is your next port of call.

Take the path leading left from the small cairn and follow it for about eight minutes, to a junction. Here take the path heading sharp left to Judas Peak (**3h05min**). From this summit (758m/2486ft) you can see for miles in all directions. A quick perusal of the map will soon tell you what you're looking at, but it will not prepare you for its breathtaking beauty. This is a wonderful spot from which to overlook the Atlantic coastline, its beaches, bays and promontories, and the mountains rising from sea-swept rocks — from Hout Bay to Lion's Head and northwards into the hazy distance.

There is a large cave under the peak, facing south — a

good place to have lunch if the sun is too hot or the wind too strong. Then move on: return to the fork below the summit and continue straight on. The path soon heads southwest and reaches a cairn a little to the right. Take the path that goes *past* it, *not* the path going left (which peters out within a few paces). The main path soon turns left (**3h15min**) and descends to the upper reaches of Llandudno Ravine, to a cairn marking the junction of several paths. You can take the path to the right from the cairn, but it is narrow and exposed at one point, where some scrambling is necessary. Its surface is also soft and easily eroded. It is better to take the main path; this turns sharp right *before* reaching the cairn (after about seven minutes of descent). It too is in poor condition, but wide and stony, better able to withstand heavy traffic. The two paths meet further down, at another cairn below a high buttress (**3h50min**).

This is rough country with spectacular rock all around you; the sea is still far below. Once the paths have joined they descend to a broad ledge going south along the western face of Hout Bay Corner — one of several ledges between sandstone cliffs. From the corner (**4h10min**) the path descends the mountainside again, scrambling down two layers of rock (turn right each time you reach the bottom) and then down to a ridge overlooking Llandudno. The path leaves the ridge just before reaching its nose, dropping to the left. Soon after, the path reaches two rows of pine trees sloping down the mountainside and descends alongside them, before reaching a crossing path (**4h 30min**).

This is the upper contour path. Return to your car at Suikerbossie from here (**4h45min**).

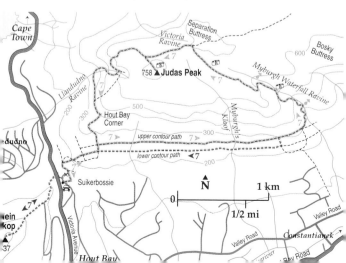

8 NOORDHOEKPIEK FROM CHAPMAN'S PEAK DRIVE

See also photograph page 81   **Distance/time**: 12km/7.4mi; 4h45min

Grade: strenuous. The initial climb is not particularly arduous, but there are several steeper ones later on, between Noordhoekpiek and Blackburn Ravine. Avoid windy days; sections of path across the escarpment are exposed to the wind. Start out early, too, so that most of the climbing can be done in the shade. Climb 800m/2625ft.

Equipment: walking boots, jersey, sunhat, waterproofs, picnic, water; suncream and long-sleeved shirt in sunny weather. Note that there is only one source of water on this walk, near the bottom of Blackburn Ravine (about two-thirds of the way round).

How to get there and return: 🚌 Take the route to Chapman's Peak described in Car tour 2 on pages 15-16 and park in the lay-by on the left, at the last right-hand bend before reaching the top of Chapman's Peak Drive. If you can muster two cars, you might like to leave the second car as described in Alternative walk 2 below, omitting the lower traverse from Blackburn Ravine.

Alternative walks

1   Chapman's Peak. 5km/3mi; 1h45min. Grade, equipment and access as main walk. Climb 438m/1435ft. Follow the main walk to the saddle (24min), then turn right at the first path. You climb past Lower Chapman's Peak on a good path which soon reaches the summit of Chapman's Peak (593m/1945ft). The view from the top is almost as good as the one from Noordhoekpiek. Return by the same route.

2   Lower traverse to Blackburn Ravine. 6km/3.7mi; 1h55min. Moderate. Equipment and access as main walk. Climb 150m/500ft. Note that two cars are needed unless you don't mind retracing your steps; leave the second car at the lay-by at the foot of Blackburn Ravine. (After driving out of Hout Bay on Chapman's Peak Drive, the road winds past three lay-bys on the left. The first two provide access to the old fort; park at the *third*, at the end of a track leading to Blackburn Ravine. Only the lay-by is open to traffic, not the track.) Follow the main walk to the saddle (24min), then turn left at the cross-path one minute later and follow the traverse in the opposite direction from that described in main walk. Walk down to the lay-by at the foot of Blackburn Ravine by continuing down the right-hand side of the stream after crossing it at the small dam; the path soon widens to an overgrown jeep track. Look out for a good short cut path descending steeply to the left after the track bends right into open country — the entrance to the path is marked by cairns, about 500m/yds beyond the bend. From the dam to the lay-by takes about 25min.

Noordhoekpiek hardly qualifies as a peak at all by any normal yardstick. Without the large cairn built on its summit you would hardly notice its existence when approaching from the east. In fact, even its steep western face is difficult to separate from the cliffs on either side. But when it comes to position, the peak has few equals. Lying about 3km to the south of Constantiaberg, its rocky face set implacably towards the Atlantic Ocean, the summit (754m/2475ft) forms the highest point of a long escarpment rising high above the narrow shore. The view from the top is one of the most spectacular in the peninsula.

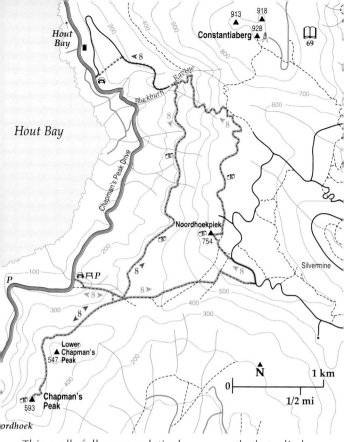

This walk follows a relatively easy path that climbs across the peak's southern flank before approaching the top across a plateau sloping down to the east. The path then continues across a series of buttresses and ravines to the north, before descending Blackburn Ravine and traversing back to the starting point. The scenery from the summits of the buttresses is very fine indeed: a contrasting mix of steep ravines strewn with rock, flora and bush in the foreground, set against the rolling waves of the Atlantic and the shores of the peninsula stretching down to the southern horizon.

The walk begins at the left of a concrete picnic table in the lay-by. The path climbs through thick undergrowth at first, before becoming stony and eroded as it makes for a saddle lying between Chapman's Peak to the right and Noordhoekpiek to the left. Keep straight on when you reach the saddle (**24min**), passing a path off to the right. *(But for Alternative walk 1, turn right here.)* Ignore another crossing path one minute later. *(But for Alternative walk 2 turn left at this crossroad.)* Continue to a flat outcrop of rock, where you keep left (instead of taking the more

65

Protea repens
(sugar bush protea)

obvious path diagonally to the right). Soon afterwards the path bends to the left and begins to climb away from the saddle. Keep left again at a fork (**30min**) and then continue through a sheltered hollow and out on to the southern slope of Noordhoekpiek.

After rising straight uphill for a while, the path begins a long steady climb to the right, pushing through thick protea bush before reaching a sloping plateau at the top. There the path becomes a sandy track, soon arriving at a wide jeep track cutting back to the left (**1h25min**). Turn left on the track, and then go left again at a stone pillar at the side of the track. The cairn at the top of Noordhoekpiek is now clearly visible on the skyline ahead. As the path begins to circumnavigate the cairn to the right, take a path forking left which leads straight to the summit (**1h40min**). This is a good place to rest for a while, and quench your thirst, for the view is considerable. Constantiaberg, with its tell-tale TV mast, lies nearby to the north, and Chapman's Peak — now well below you — to the south. The mountains of the southern peninsula march raggedly away to the south, while the town of Hout Bay nestles behind its attractive harbour like a picture postcard. Boats of all shapes and sizes plough up and down the bay, and a forest of tall-masted yachts lies anchored to the harbour wall. To the left of the harbour, the Sentinel rises sheer from the sea under the shadow of its somnolent northern neighbours, Karbonkelberg and Suther Peak, the latter collared by white sand dunes sloping down to the northern outskirts of the town.

Having taken your fill of the scenery, walk down a path to the north of the ascent path and rejoin the path skirting the peak — now going north. You soon cross a jeep track; your continuing path is marked by a small cairn a few paces to the left. The path continues north, keeping close to the western escarpment as it undulates across a series of rugged buttresses and deep ravines. This is spectacular country — mountain scenery at its best — relieved by frequent glimpses of the sea and the western coastline. Every now and again (over your left shoulder) you will catch glimpses of Kommitjie Lighthouse, its white silhouette rising beyond the eastern flank of Chapman's Peak.

The path eventually drops down to the saddle below Constantiaberg, where you follow a broad sandy path off to the left, to the edge of the escarpment above Blackburn Ravine (**2h40min**). This ravine is one of the biggest anywhere on these mountains, scattered with bushes, rocks and a myriad of streams. At first your route down the ravine keeps to the left in a careful series of zigzags. Then, as the ravine steepens and widens, the path contours well to the right before resuming its zigzag route downhill.

Shortly afterwards the path crosses the stream in thick woodland, returning to it a little further down — at a point where a water pipe runs downstream from a small dam above the path to the left. Leave the main path here and cross the stream just below the dam (**3h25min**). The path now climbs steadily southwards across the mountainside, before levelling out and traversing back to the saddle between Noordhoekpiek and Chapman's Peak (**4h30min**). It is a long traverse which winds its way round the feet of the buttresses and ravines you crossed earlier, at the top of the escarpment. The path gives way to one wide prospect after another, as well as some intriguing insights into the precipitous depths below — vivid illustrations of the dangers of descending unknown ravines!

The saddle is broad and easy to recognise from your earlier encounter with it on the way up; the paths are clear and wide. The descent to the right, from the saddle down to the lay-by, takes about 15 minutes (**4h45min**). But take care: the loose stone on the surface of the path is a greater hazard on the way down than on the way up.

Hout Bay from Chapman's Peak Drive. From left to right: the Sentinel, Karbonkelberg, Suther Peak and Little Lion's Head

9 CONSTANTIABERG FROM TOKAI ARBORETUM

Distance/time: 14km/8.7mi; 4h30min

Grade: strenuous. The climb, while never particularly steep, is prolonged. Climb 850m/2790ft.

Equipment: walking boots or stout walking shoes, waterproofs, jersey, sunhat, picnic, plenty of water; suncream, long-sleeved shirt in sunny weather. There is no water on the way up and little on the way down.

How to get there and return: 🚌 Follow Car tour 1, but turn left at the end of Newlands Avenue instead of going straight ahead. Follow the main road out on to the 'Blue Route' (M3) and leave it at the exit to Tokai, the junction before the motorway ends (11km). Turn right at the bottom of the slip road and keep going along a dead-straight road (Tokai Road), across a roundabout and straight on again until the road comes to a bumpy end at a large mansion behind iron gates (Tokai Manor). Turn left here and follow a gravel track round to the right where it soon comes to an end at an informal car park sheltered by tall trees next to Tokai Arboretum.

Short walk: Circuit round Tokai Arboretum. 1.2km/0.7mi; 25min. Easy. Access as main walk. The well-signposted, anti-clockwise route starts a few paces beyond the entrance to the arboretum and passes a fascinating variety of trees from all over the world — many of them clearly labelled. The path ends close to the museum, just below the entrance.

Alternative walk: Elephant's Eye and Princess Waterfall. 10km/6.2mi; 3h. Grade, equipment, access as main walk. Climb 600m/1970ft. Follow the main walk to the Elephant's Eye (1h35min) and then return to the junction first encountered at 1h20min. Here continue straight ahead instead of turning left (the way you came). On reaching a cairn with a signpost to the waterfall (1h50min), turn left and pick up the notes for the main walk from just after the 3h27min-point, to reach the falls and end the walk.

This walk is nearer to fell-walking than most of the walks described in this book: almost no rock, and plenty of trees and open greenery. After passing through Tokai Arboretum, the route — known as the 'Elephant's Eye path' — heads through a thick pine plantation on the eastern slopes of Constantiaberg. Above the trees a mountainous 'brow' looks from a distance like an elephant's eye.

Book in at the gate to the arboretum (Tokai is a variety of Hungarian grape once grown in the area). **Start out** by walking through the trees along the main track for a few hundred metres/yards, until the first 'elephant' sign points along a path going right. Take this path and climb steadily until you cross a jeep track. This crossing is the first of about eight as the path short cuts the jeep tracks criss-crossing the mountainside. Apart from two junctions further up (both staggered a little to the right) the crossings are straight-forward: just follow the elephant's trunk. The wide, hard-baked earthen path is overshadowed by tall pines and occasional groups of gum trees.

After climbing for **1h** the path comes to an end at a contour path separating the plantation from the steep mountainside above; now the countryside at last opens out.

Familiar plains and mountains roll out to the eastern and
northeastern horizons, while in the foreground the eastern
flanks of Constantiaberg lead the eye towards Table Mountain further away to the north. Straight above you, high up
to the right, you can see the cave that forms the Elephant's
Eye, surmounted by the arc of its brow. The *fynbos* above
the path is lush and green — in brilliant contrast to the dark
dry forest below.

Your route lies to the left along the shaded contour path.
After a few hundred paces it re-enters the trees and begins
to climb, zigzagging steadily up a steep incline before
emerging into sunlight once more, breathing more easily
as it wanders slowly to the top of a brow. As the view
widens out, the path reaches a junction (**1h20min**), where
an elephant sign points to the right and another sign points
the way towards a waterfall 1km/0.6mi over to the left.
*(This is where the Alternative walk heads for the waterfall
after returning from the Elephant's Eye.)* You are now standing at the mouth of a long wide valley running below the
southern flank of Constantiaberg, which slopes up to the
right. Further to the left, more mountains rise, with a broad
winding track climbing steadily towards the summit of
Noordhoekpiek, the highest point on the western horizon.

Take the path to the right, narrow and overgrown with
tall *fynbos*. Soon you arrive at a fork, where another elephant sign is hidden behind a low bush. From here there
are two possible routes. The main route goes right and
climbs to a fire-watcher's hut on a high rock overlooking
the eastern plains. From the hut the path switches left and
makes its way up the mountainside once more, passing to
the left of the Elephant's Eye. A shorter option is to take the
path going left at the fork. Both routes cross a jeep track

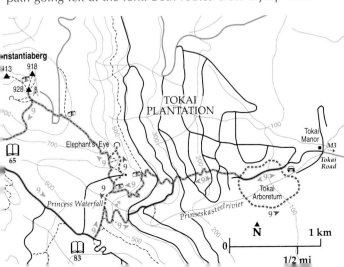

leading up to the hut. If you choose the long way round you might as well carry on and visit the Elephant's Eye (**1h35min**) — the way is clear enough after you've passed the fire-watcher's hut. You can leave the 'eye' afterwards along a short ledge to the left, above the floor of the cave, rejoining the main path a hundred paces further on. But the cave is not all that attractive: it looks better from a distance. Inside, it is large, dirty and featureless, its dusty floor rising steeply into the dark interior. Its drab appearance aside, the cave used to be called 'Prinseskasteel' (Princess's Castle), after a Hottentot princess who was reputed to have hidden there a few hundred years ago — the only member of her tribe to survive a battle with a rival tribe. A nearby stream (the Prinseskasteelrivier) is said to have been fed by her tears ever since. You will cross it on the way back — it's the stream with the waterfall.

The path now climbs diagonally across the southern flank of the mountain, sometimes easily and sometimes with difficulty — once offering a glimpse of the mast at the top, looking deceptively close. Shortly after this first view of the mast, the path emerges on the summit of the ridge behind the elephant's head (**1h45min**). The mast can be clearly seen now as the path ahead goes straight for it,

rising gently as it closes in on the mast and summit. There is a fork in the path after some steady climbing. While the prong to the right *looks* like the obvious way forward, take the path straight ahead: it is more direct. Although the way is steep, it soon emerges on a small plateau and arrives without warning at a tarred road. Cross the road and pick up the path again about twenty paces to the left (in a narrow cleft). Shortly afterwards the path recrosses the road higher up; this time the continuing path is uphill to the right and marked with a cairn.

You're almost there: over the next brow the path finally reaches the TV relay station, a cluster of low buildings at the foot of the mast. The latter is very tall indeed, secured to the ground with long wire hawsers set into concrete blocks. The whole complex is surrounded by a sturdy wire fence. The path continues alongside the southern perimeter fence, reaching the far corner-post at the top of a short incline. Here a strong path goes off left and another heads to the right. Take the right-hand path, climbing alongside the western fence for a short distance, before turning left and scrambling to the summit (**2h20min**).

There are three beacons at the top, the first being the highest (928m/3045ft). Given a fine day, the climb is worth every step, for the prospect from here is very wide indeed. If you look north, the stone igloo forming Maclear's Beacon stands out clearly on the skyline — on the right-hand side of the table. To the left, the heads of the Twelve Apostles, rising in a line on the western escarpment, are so close it seems you can almost touch them. The whole of Table Mountain is laid out before you like a contoured map. In the foreground to the south lies Noordhoekpiek, with Chapman's Peak to the right and Hout Bay nestling in the valley below. The Sentinel, a sheer rock, guards the entrance to the harbour, with Karbonkelberg high up to the right. To the southeast, beyond Simon's Town and the mountains behind it, you can pick out Judas Peak (a *second* one — one betrayal was not enough apparently!) and Die Boer, close to Cape Point. The wide sweep of False Bay, the long arc of the distant mountains, and the limitless ocean with its slow-moving ships and treacherous foam-flecked rocks complete the scene.

Far left: the traverse above Tokai Plantation, looking north into a steep gully below the Elephant's Eye. Left: view south to the Elephant's Eye (top) — its 'brow' is to the right, with the mast on Constantiaberg to the left; Table Mountain from the summit of Constantiaberg (middle); Constantiaberg from the slopes of Suther Peak (bottom).

You can walk on to the other two beacons too, if you have time: good paths lead to both from the first beacon. You can also explore the path going right at the corner of the fence when you climb down to it again. It meanders along at the foot of the peak for a short distance before rising to a labyrinth of caves. This feature is known locally as Olifantsgat (Elephant's Arse). Inside, there are thick needles of rock reaching from floor to roof — looking like stalagmites and stalactites, but formed by weathered rock rather than deposits of lime. It takes about 10 minutes to walk there and back.

After regaining the main path at the corner-post, keep walking alongside the southern fence for about sixty paces and then fork right on a clear path meandering diagonally across a sloping plateau. At the far edge, the path veers right and wends a cautious way down a steep slope — to a broad saddle looking across Hout Bay to the Atlantic (**2h55min**). This is the summit of Blackburn Ravine, lying at the head of the long wide valley separating Noordhoek-piek from Constantiaberg. Turn away from the ravine, to the left, and follow a slowly-climbing jeep track. When you join another jeep track (the main track from Silvermine to the top of Noordhoekpiek), carry on in the same direction until you descend a steep incline where the track is paved on both sides with concrete strips (just after passing the track leading back to the fire-watcher's hut). As the concrete ends, take a broad path going left (**3h20min**).

After about seven minutes (**3h27min**; soon after returning to the edge of the forest), you come to a ramshackle cairn on the right with a notice next to it pointing to a waterfall. Cut back right here and descend a broad path through the trees. After several long zigzags the waterfall appears in front of you; the cliff behind it is very wide, with a number of horizontal ledges on its face. This is an impressive spectacle after the rains have set in — a river of water thundering down a pitted face of dark mottled sandstone.

Shortly afterwards the path descends to a three-way junction of jeep tracks (**3h45min**). Walk over to the left for a few paces, then take the right-hand fork which descends steadily for some distance before passing another track cutting back to the right. After this junction the path traverses northwards until it comes to one of the elephant crossings. Wait until you see the elephant sign before turning downhill to the right (an earlier path is a short cut and should be avoided to prevent erosion). Now return to the arboretum by your outward path (**4h30min**).

10 ST JAMES PEAK, KALK BAY PEAK AND ECHO VALLEY

Distance/time: 8km/5mi; 3h20min

Grade: moderate, with a short climb at the outset and then a pleasant amble in gently-undulating countryside. Climb 500m/1640ft.

Equipment: walking boots (preferable) or stout shoes, sunhat, jersey, waterproofs, picnic, water; suncream, long-sleeved shirt in sunny weather

How to get there and return: 🚗 Follow Car tour 1 (pages 11-12) to Boyes Drive in Lakeside. Keep on this road until you reach an area with lamp-posts on either side — just over 5km along. Park close to house No 110 (remember to park on the left — it is against the law to park facing the traffic). Or 🚂 to/from St James (for departures telephone: 405 3871). Walk up one of the roads and steps leading to Boyes Drive (Sandhurst or St James). Once on Boyes Drive find your way to house No 110.

Short walk: Traverse to Muizenberg and return via Boyes Drive. 4km/2.5mi; 1h20min. Moderate. Wear ordinary walking clothes and stout shoes. Access as main walk. Climb 50m/160ft. Follow the main walk for 25min, then head gradually downhill on the path as it contours above Boyes Drive. When you arrive at a point above a huge block of flats that dominates the rest of Muizenberg, turn right downhill on a steeply-stepped path and return to the starting point by walking up Boyes Drive.

Alternative walk: St James Peak, Kalk Bay Peak and the Spes Bona Valley. 7km/4.3mi; 3h. Grade, equipment, access as main walk. Climb 450m/1475ft. Follow the main walk to the Spes Bona Valley (2h05min), then turn left instead of right. Go down to the jeep track at the bottom of the valley, turn right along it, and follow it to its end. Then pick up the main walk again at the 2h56min-point (at the left of the track), to walk down the traverse back to your starting point.

Shorter alternative walk: St James Peak and Nellie's Pool. 5km/3mi; 2h. Grade, equipment, access as main walk. Climb 350m/1150ft. Follow the main walk to Nellie's Pool (1h20min), then turn left on the jeep track instead of crossing it. You descend to the traverse at the end of the main walk: pick up the main walk at the 2h56min-point and follow it to the end.

The southern peninsula is good walking country — not as grand as further north perhaps, but it doesn't suffer on that account. You can get to the top much sooner for one thing, saving your breath for the walking rather than the climbing. For another, the area has its own atmosphere, restful and quiet: the sea is close and the city far away. Several of the easier walks described in this book are located in this area — this one included.

This route runs anti-clockwise from a point about 100m/330ft above sea level. It starts with a steady climb to St James Peak (422m/1385ft) and then follows an undulating path across a number of valleys and ridges to the top of Kalk Bay Peak (516m/1692ft). From there the path finds its way through a natural amphitheatre and returns to its starting point via Echo Valley and a long traverse down to Boyes Drive. The route is marked by caves, weathered rock formations and a small and dark mountain pool. If you start early enough, it is a comfortable morning's walk.

73

The path begins next to a gully on the opposite side of the road from No 110 Boyes Drive. Follow it to the left for a few paces, then fork right. Now your well-constructed path winds up the mountainside in a series of climbs, zigzags and traverses, its main purpose being to contour north — to the right. (Note that two early side-paths going right and left soon peter out.) Ignore a path going down to the right at the end of a long traverse across the steep mountainside (**25min**). *(But for the Short walk go right here.)* The path climbs up to the left and within five minutes arrives at a four-way junction — just beyond another path going left. The mountainside levels out here, a wide valley opening out to the left and a much steeper gorge going down to the right — St James Kloof. The mountain is thickly covered in undergrowth, making it impossible to make any headway except on the path.

Keep straight on at this junction: the crossing path leads up the Mimetes Valley from Boyes Drive. Your path continues climbing gradually, with a couple of short paths going right to viewpoints. After a long curve to the left, the path forks: the left prong heads for the front face of St James Peak (its summit is just above you), but the main path approaches the summit from the right. Take the main path and, after a little easy scrambling near the top, reach the

View across False Bay to the Hottentots-Holland range

peak in about **55min**. The summit, covered with bare flat rock, is marked by a beacon — lean up against it while having your photograph taken, to heighten your sense of achievement... Then take in the fine views across False Bay — down its western coastline and eastwards to the beautiful mountains of the Boland which stride across the horizon in a huge arc, silhouetted against a fading sky. The seaside town to your right is Fish Hoek, while Simon's Town, the famous naval base, lies a little further south — you can see its harbour walls reaching out to sea. Immediately to the northeast lies Muizenberg, its southeastern flank sloping steeply down to its urban namesake.

Head west from the beacon, following a path that threads its way through the rock — a continuation of the path that went for the front face earlier on. After about five minutes the path forks again: keep left and make for the highest point of the ridge, a little further on (457m/1499ft). The path descends gradually on the other side, passing a path coming in from the left. When you reach the next path cutting back sharply to the left, turn onto it and climb a low ridge. This wide sandy path scatters in all directions as it tops the ridge. There is an interesting cave about 30 paces to the left called Muizenberg Cave; it dips darkly below the overhanging rock.

The main path descends the far side of the ridge and soon reaches a narrow path forking right. Unlikely though it may seem, that's the path you should follow: it soon meanders through thick undergrowth to a dark pond: Nellie's Pool (**1h20min**). It is a very pretty spot, edged with lush green banks. (But no matter how warm the day, do *not* throw yourself into the water unless you really enjoy being covered from head to foot in black mud.)

The path skirts the pond on its far bank and joins a jeep track a few paces further on, at the edge of a wide valley. *(The Shorter alternative walk turns left here.)* Take the path that continues on the far side of the track; after crossing the valley, it joins another track. Cross this track too and continue along the path (at the side of a stone pillar). A quick glance at the map tells you that the ridge in front of you leads to Kalk Bay Peak. The path ascending it is a wide one, a mixture of sand and rock. Keep left when the path forks, and veer right after passing another path going to a viewpoint on the left.

The path climbs steeply as it bends to the right, soon reaching the top of the ridge, which it follows in a westerly direction to a beacon at the far end. This is the topmost point of the mountain, standing some 516m/1692ft above sea level (**2h**). It is also one of the best viewpoints on the peninsula, looking out to all points of the compass. On the northwestern horizon you can see the heads of the Twelve Apostles forming a long line heading towards the topmost summit of Table Mountain — the table itself a long flat line across the northern skyline. To the south of The Apostles, Constantiaberg and Noordhoekpiek form a long undulating bridge to Chapman's Peak on the western horizon. Further south still, a wide sandy beach drifts down to Kommitjie and its familiar lighthouse, a lone white figure looking across the vast expanse of the southern Atlantic. The rest of the horizon is the same as ever: the mountains of the peninsula to the south — with Simon's Town's docks sheltering behind a natural headland on the western shore of False Bay — and range upon range of mountains marching across the eastern and northeastern skylines, from Hangklip on the far side of False Bay to Simonsberg on the northeastern skyline, partly hiding the more distant ranges on the far horizons.

From the beacon, walk back to the main path curling southwards and follow it down to the next valley: Spes Bona (**2h05min**), a succinct Portuguese translation of '[Cape of] Good Hope'. Turn right at a path coming up the valley *(but for the Alternative walk turn left)* and then go left at a crossroad shortly afterwards. The path climbs over a shallow ridge, crossing another path en route, and descends somewhat hesitantly into a hollow down to the right. There are several caves in the rocks on this descent, including one to the left under a grove of trees and bushes — with a path leading to it. The main path veers right at this point (although the path to the cave looks stronger); it then clambers down through a narrow gap between large rocks. At the bottom of the path, turn right at a T-junction. You pass another grove of trees standing in the shadow of a deeply-serrated wall of dark weathered rocks on the right. Immediately beyond the grove, the path enters a natural amphitheatre — a circular enclosure almost entirely bordered by a tumble of rocks and trees (**2h20min**).

Walk further into the amphitheatre before taking a broad path leading off to the left; it will take you down into the steep-sided valley below — Echo Valley, full of trees and grottos, one of the best-known of the peninsula's gorges. There is a gathering of the clans here, paths coming in from all directions, but the path you want is clear enough: head straight down the valley to the left. (You can either join the path by the main junction near the head of the valley to the right or take an earlier path to the left which joins the main one soon afterwards.)

It takes about 30 minutes to walk down Echo Valley, heavily shaded with evergreen trees at first, then open to the sky further down. At the bottom there is a stone pillar with Echo Valley engraved on it (**2h55min**). Turn left at this pillar and cross a stream; a grove of trees shades the path on the far side (**2h56min**). *(The Alternative and Short alternative walks rejoin the main walk here.)* Beyond the trees the path widens into a track and arrives at a junction where you turn right. This path drops down towards False Bay to begin with and then veers left and traverses the mountainside above Boyes Drive, eventually reaching the road at your starting point (**3h20min**).

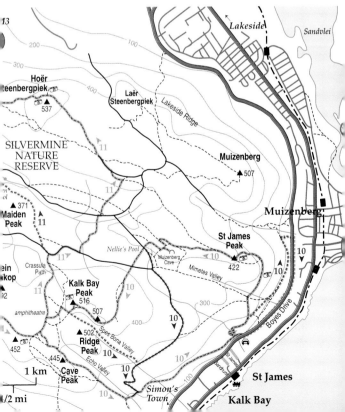

11 SILVERMINE'S NATURAL AMPHITHEATRE FROM THE OU KAAPSEWEG

See map on pages 76-77

Distance/time: 11km/6.8mi; 3h35min

Grade: moderate. Climb 400m/1300ft.

Equipment: walking boots or stout shoes, waterproofs, jersey, picnic, water, sunhat; long-sleeved shirt and sun-cream in sunny weather

How to get there and return: 🚗 Follow Car tour 1 (pages 11-12) to the end of the 'Blue Route', then turn right. Bear left at the next junction and join the M64. This road is known as the Ou Kaapseweg (Old Cape Road) and forms a pass across the mountains. At the summit of the pass a road goes off right to the northern Silvermine area. Keep to the main road and turn left about 800m beyond this junction, into a car park under tall pines. Leave nothing of value in the car; the car park's position under the trees sometimes attracts thieves, especially when there are few people about.

Alternative walk: The amphitheatre and Maiden Pool. 7km/4.3mi; 2h 30min. Grade, equipment, access as main walk. Climb 200m/650ft. Follow the main walk to the jeep track at the bottom of the Crassula Path (1h45min), then turn left instead of right. Some 60 paces after this turning, bear right on a good sandy path which runs steadily downhill, crosses a low ridge, and then continues downhill — to the left of Maiden Pool. Shortly after, the path reaches a jeep track: turn right here, then go left on another jeep track almost immediately. This is the track you took on the outward leg from the car park; retrace your steps.

Silvermine Nature Reserve (setting for Walks 10 to 13) derives its name from a fruitless exploration for silver in 1687. The remnants of the mine still exist, further down the Ou Kaapseweg on the way to Fish Hoek. You will see them from a distance soon after beginning this walk. The pass forms the boundary between the reserve's southern and northern sections. As the road is very much higher than Boyes Drive (Walk 10), this walk is relatively easy — without the steepness that characterises the False Bay edge. The countryside is similar, in that it comprises a series of rocky peaks and ridges cleft by deep sloping valleys, but it is gentler country, its eyes cast inland instead of out to sea.

To start the walk, find your way to the southern edge of the car park, where there is a line of short timber posts (the road will be behind you). Here take the jeep track going right (south) and follow it out of the trees, with the slopes of Wolfkop on your left. After about **15min** along the track, a path goes off right and drops down to a waterfall. Take this path and follow it across the top of the waterfall (the path is navigable almost all year round). On the far side you meet another jeep track, where you again turn right. (Note that if you miss the waterfall path, you can take the jeep track going right at the first fork and you will arrive at the same point: the path is simply a picturesque short cut.)

78

The track now circumnavigates Maiden Peak to the left before arriving at another fork (**30min**). Keep right again; the track soon deteriorates into an overgrown path. It recovers its shape soon afterwards, but is still too overgrown to serve as a jeep track. After traversing right for a while under Klein Tuinkop, the path loses all pretence of being a jeep track and begins a gradual rise to the left, running above a wide valley on the right (Klein Tuinkloof — 'Little Garden Ravine'). Note the view down the Silvermine Valley as the path approaches Klein Tuinkloof. The stream runs well below the Ou Kaapseweg. You will notice two tracks running down towards the stream from the far side of the valley: they appear to connect with a path leading to the path you are on (the junction being closer to the waterfall.) Next to those tracks, just below the road, is the long-abandoned silver mine.

As the valley narrows, the path joins its centre and climbs steadily to its head (**1h15min**). From the saddle a view across False Bay opens up, straight down Echo Valley, flanked by Cave Peak to the right and Ridge Peak to the left. Behind you lies the Atlantic, with views to Constantiaberg, Noordhoekpiek and Chapman's Peak. Just beyond the saddle the path reaches another path coming down from Cave Peak: keep left here and cross the head of Echo Valley, passing three more paths joining from the valley. Your path then climbs the lower slopes of Ridge Peak and forks left into a level area almost completely surrounded by bushes, rocks and low cliffs — a natural amphitheatre. This is an excellent place to take a break and explore some of its nooks and crannies, but beware of deep

Fine examples of weathered rock, for which Silvermine is renowned, near the summit of Klein Tuinkop. Constantiaberg rises in the north.

potholes at the base of the cliffs opposite the point where you came in.

Your exit path skirts the left-hand perimeter of the amphitheatre and climbs out of it, still bearing left. You reach another saddle, between Ridge Peak and Klein-Tuinkop (470m/1540ft above sea level and about 210m/690ft above the waterfall). From here a good path takes you in a steady descent towards a jeep track in a wide valley some distance away to the north. This is the Crassula Path, presumably named for the crimson flowers which bloom here in late spring and early summer. Once the path reaches the track (**1h45min**), turn right and follow the track uphill as it bends left and then right. *(But for the Alternative walk go left at this junction.)* A few hundred paces beyond the second bend, a path marked by a small cairn heads towards a low outcrop of rock on your left. Take this path: it goes round the rock to the left and then continues downhill on the far side, to a nameless stream which flows into the Silvermine River below the waterfall. From the stream the path rises to another jeep track (**2h**): turn right briefly, then pick up your path on the far side of the track, crossing two more paths.

Your path continues to rise until it reaches a fork, where you turn left and continue to a wider path going left and then to a rough jeep track which you join at an angle — still climbing (**2h30min**). The track narrows soon afterwards and changes to a sandy path which winds its way to the top of Hoër Steenbergpiek (Higher Stone Peak) — the highest point of the walk (537m/1761ft). The outlook to the north and east from this peak is extensive and impressive, the terrain dropping down quickly in both directions. Both Table Mountain and Constantiaberg seem close on the northern horizon; the eastern horizon, beyond the vineyards and False Bay, consists of a wide arc of distant mountains: Cecil Rhodes' hinterland.

On your descent, turn left where a path goes off right to the edge of the escarpment and follow the broad sandy path all the way down to the bottom of the peak. (Or first walk to the edge of the escarpment, where the view reveals a detailed map of town and country — a network of roads, lagoons and waterways leading down to False Bay at the mouth of the Dieprivier near Muizenberg.)

Once at the bottom of the peak, you can either keep ahead to a jeep track which runs left along the pine plantation at the start of the walk, or take the path contouring a little above the track before descending (**3h35min**).

12 NORTH SILVERMINE CIRCUIT TO NOORDHOEKPIEK

See also photograph page 67   **Distance/time**: 6.5km/4mi; 2h40min

Grade: strenuous on the switchback ascent to Noordhoekpiek, otherwise easy-moderate. Climb 480m/1575ft. This is a different and easier version of Walk 8, especially recommended for those who appreciate fine scenery but don't feel the urge to court an early death in an attempt to find it. Avoid windy or misty days, when the switchback could be dangerous. If your party comprises people of different abilities, the slower walkers could take the Alternative walk: part company where the jeep track forks (35min) and meet up again at the summit of Noordhoekpiek.

Equipment: walking boots or stout shoes, sunhat, jersey, waterproofs, picnic or barbecue, water; long-sleeved shirt, suncream in a sunny weather

How to get there and return: 🚗 Follow Car tour 1 (pages 11-12) to the end of the 'Blue Route', then turn right. Fork left at the next turning, onto the M64, the Ou Kaapseweg (Old Cape Road). Once at the summit of the pass, turn right on a road towards the Silvermine Forest Reserve and follow it past a picnic area and through a toll gate, to a car park about 2km from the gate. *Note that the gates are open between 8am and 6pm.*

Short walk: Circular walk through the Silvermine Valley. 2km/1.2mi; 30min. Easy. Wear stout shoes. Access as main walk. Follow the main walk along the right bank of the dam and then right towards the jeep track. There is a path going left before the track is reached, marked by red paint on a rock. Follow it, and stick to it as it wanders around within the circular jeep track and returns to the car park along the left-hand bank of the dam.

Alternative walk: Noordhoekpiek: easier circuit. 5.5km/3.4mi; 2h05min. Moderate; equipment and access as main walk. This version eliminates the switchback ascent. Follow the main walk for 35min, then turn left instead of right at the fork in the jeep track. Your track winds steadily uphill towards Noordhoekpiek. Near the top, where the main track turns left (1h), follow a track going straight ahead. Turn left again at the first path you come to, and climb to the peak (marked by a large cairn; 1h05min). Then pick up the main walk at the 1h35min point to return.

This is not exactly an 'armchair walk', but it's a much less energetic way of reaching the summit of Noordhoekpiek than the route described in Walk 8. Starting at an altitude of 440m instead of 154m, the hike combines the best of both worlds: the spectacular seascapes described in Walk 8 and the gentler landscapes of the Silvermine area. The main walk describes an anti-clockwise circuit above the valley at the centre of the reserve with its pine forests and reservoir. It skirts the southern slopes of Constantiaberg on the way up and then winds up and down the

North of the Noordhoek summit; note the thick fynbos.

switchback of buttresses and gorges plunging down the Atlantic escarpment to the west. After climbing to the top of Noordhoekpiek, one of the grandest viewpoints in the peninsula, the route returns by a series of paths wandering along a ridge high above the valley.

To start the hike, walk to the northernmost end of the tarred car park and cross a wooden bridge. On the far side cross the jeep track and head into the trees on a path. You soon reach a wall at the southern end of a reservoir set in a picturesque valley of mixed pines and *fynbos*. Keep along the right (eastern) shore of the reservoir, with a picnic area on your right. As the path begins bending left towards a small bridge at the northern end of the reservoir, fork right and follow a narrower path to another, broader path, which takes you towards the jeep track circling the valley.

Cross the track and continue to a higher track running parallel with the first. Turn left uphill here. The track negotiates several hairpin bends before rising even further on a section paved by two concrete strips. (Several paths short cut the hairpin bends, but all are very steep and stony; it's easier to keep to the track.) Ignore a track going right to a fire hut at the top of the concrete strips. The gradient levels out once the concrete is cleared, the track eventually reaching a fork (**35min**). *(The Alternative walk branches left here.)* You are now walking in a high valley with Constantiaberg on the right and Noordhoekpiek on the left.

Keep right at the fork and continue on a very rough track for another five minutes, until the track is pinned together by timber poles. You are now near the top of Blackburn Ravine, with the path to the summit of Constantiaberg going off right a little further on. A few paces *before* the first pole, take the path heading uphill to the left; it climbs some 180m/590ft, to a nameless peak overlooking the Atlantic — the first of many viewpoints on a series of steep switchbacks heading for Noordhoekpiek. (Walk 8 tackles this switchback the other way.) The designer of the path must have taken a degree in drama as well as architecture, for it climbs every conceivable peak and plunges down every available abyss on its short journey across the escarpment.

The summit of Noordhoekpiek is marked by a large cairn which can be seen from a distance. It is approached on a path going off right from a much broader and sandier one which skirts the peak to the left. The summit (**1h35min**) stands some 754m/2473ft above sea level and gives way to a 360° panorama of great beauty. The little harbour at your feet belongs to the fishing town of Hout Bay and the lighthouse along the distant southern shore stands on the far side of Kommitjie. Glimpses of Simon's Town, the naval base, can be seen on the False Bay coast to the south — under the shadow of Simonsberg.

Rejoin the sandy path by closing the triangle of paths from the summit, and bear right. Then, when the path forks, go left on a cart track which soon joins a jeep track. Turn left for about 50 paces, before taking a path to the right. This path descends gradually amidst an area of rich *fynbos* — heather and protea in particular, with reeds and grasses down to the left. The path ends at a sharp bend on the jeep track, which you now follow downhill to the next right-hand bend, a few hundred metres/yards further on. Here go left uphill on a broad path. At the summit of a nearby ridge (**2h05min**) you meet a crossroad: turn right and follow the path gradually down the spine of the ridge, high above the valley to the left. This is a fine section of the walk, with a clear view of the forests and reservoir below. Keep left where a path goes right to join up with the jeep track again. You descend to rejoin the track much lower down, where it sweeps back towards the reservoir (**2h30min**). Turn left now, and either follow the track down to the car park or cross the reservoir wall about 500m/yds down the track and take your outgoing footpath (**2h40min**).

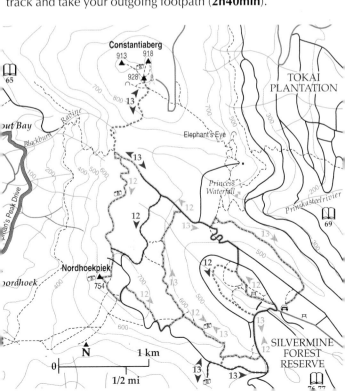

13 RIDGE CIRCUIT IN NORTH SILVERMINE

See map page 83   **Distance/time**: 5km/3mi; 2h

Grade: moderate — undulating terrain without any steep gradients; the paths are easy on the feet for most of the way. Climb 220m/720ft.

Equipment: walking boots or stout shoes, jersey, sunhat, waterproofs, picnic or barbecue, water; long-sleeved shirt, suncream in sunny weather

How to get there and return: as Walk 12, page 81

Short walk: Fire-watch circuit. 4km/2.5mi; 1h20min. Moderate. Stout shoes will suffice. Access as main walk. Climb 140m/460ft. Follow the main walk to the fork met in 20min and go left. When the path meets a jeep track, turn right. At the next junction go left. This track leads to a path that climbs to a fire-watch (45min). After visiting it, follow the track all the way back; it curls round to the left after passing the ascent path.

Alternative walk: Constantiaberg summit. 7km/4.3mi; 3h20min. Climb 490m/1610ft. Strenuous. Equipment and access as main walk. This ascent is much easier than Walk 9, as the strenuous section is relatively short. Follow the main walk to the jeep track (1h15min). Then turn left and walk up the track, keeping right at the first fork. The track deteriorates into a wide path and makes for the top of Blackburn Ravine. Just a few paces before this main path starts to descend the ravine (1h25min), take another path climbing uphill to the right, to Constantiaberg (2h). The summit rises above and to the left of a fence surrounding a TV station (if in doubt, refer to Walk 9 at the 2h20min-point). Return by the same path and rejoin the main walk where you left it — at the 1h15min point.

This fine walk will appeal to anyone whose sense of beauty exceeds the capacity of his lungs. There is some climbing to begin with (the walk starts about 440m/1445ft above sea level and rises to 660m/2165ft at its highest point), but the path isn't steep and is so full of interest that one barely notices the climb. The descent is gentle too, though the path is uneven and rocky in places. The path circles the Silvermine Valley in a clockwise direction, keeping it always in sight, but also affording more distant vistas as the path rises. One advantage of this walk (and Walk 12) is the picnic area next to the reservoir. You can either picnic along the walk or barbecue in the hearths.

To start the walk, cross the wooden bridge on the northern edge of the car park and then take the jeep track going left. The track curves left after a short while and continues past another track going right (the inner circular track). Keep ahead, gradually climbing, with a pine plantation on your left, *fynbos* to the right and the reservoir behind you. After about **12min** a footpath goes off right, its entry point marked by a picture of a *duiker* (small antelope). Take this path; it cuts back sharply and begins a diagonal ascent of the slopes to the left, soon arriving at a fork marked with another *duiker* (**20min**). *(The Short walk goes left here.)* Keep right and continue climbing until the path reaches the top of a high ridge about 220m/720ft above the valley. The scenery from here is outstanding:

Silvermine Dam from the ridge to the north, with Muizenberg behind it and the Kogelberge beyond the waters of False Bay

you can see for miles in all directions, the view of the valley with its forests and reservoir being particularly fine.

The path continues across another broad path (**45min**) and then begins to descend very gradually on the valley side of the ridge (the right), losing sight of the countryside to the west. Eventually, the path rounds the head of the valley and joins a jeep track at a stone pillar (**1h15min**). *(The Alternative walk branches left here.)*

Walk down the track to the right for about 600m/0.4mi, past a track off left to a fire-watch hut. When you get to the bottom of a steep section of track bordered by concrete strips, turn left. Follow a broad stony path for about 100m/yds, then take a narrow path to the right. This path leads up to a low ridge above the eastern edge of the valley. After walking along it for a short distance, fork abruptly left and climb over bedrock, up to the ridge. From now on the path meanders in an uncertain manner along the top of the ridge*, with pine trees to the left hiding a deep escarpment dropping down to the Dieprivier basin and the False Bay coast. Brief glimpses of this scenery can be seen through the trees from time to time.

After about 28 minutes along the ridge (**1h53min**) the path bears right and begins its descent to the track. Cross the track and join a path on the far side, to return to your car (**2h**).

---

*This ridge path peters out sometimes; you may have to retrace your steps. But you will stumble back on to it as long as you stick to the top of the ridge — and it does become clearer as the path progresses. Moreover, you never really lose sight of your starting point all the way round this circuit.

14 COASTAL WALK TO CAPE POINT

Distance 12km/7.4mi; 4h

Grade: moderate; a constantly-undulating path. Climb 500m/1640ft.

Equipment: stout shoes or walking boots, jersey, waterproofs, sunhat, picnic or barbecue, water; suncream and long-sleeved shirt in sunny weather. There is *no* shelter from the sun.

How to get there and return: 🚗 Follow Car tour 1 (pages 11-13) to the gate at the Cape of Good Hope Nature Reserve (entrance fee payable). *You will need two cars;* one parked at Cape Point and the other at the starting point of the walk, a small lay-by on the east side of the road, about 500m beyond the gate to the reserve.

Shorter walks: The length of the walk can be reduced by joining or leaving it at either Bordjiesdrif or Buffelsbaai. Both places have car parks and are served by tarred roads leading down from the main road (see map). Grade and equipment are the same as for the main walk.

This is a fine coastal walk along the False Bay side of the nature reserve. Partly mountainous and partly drifting along the shore, the path gradually reveals a wonderful variety of landscape, seascape and sky. And if you're interested in the Cape's fauna, this is the place to be — to see sea birds in particular, but plenty of other wildlife as well: buck and baboon, snakes and lizards, beetles, butterflies and spiders galore. To get the best out of it, walk here Monday to Friday: you will see a lot more than at crowded weekends. The area can also become very hot during summer; spring is by far the best time to visit the reserve.

Towards the end of the walk, as the path rises to the spine of the peninsula, the ocean as well as the bay becomes visible. The calm waters of the latter are overtaken by the rolling foam of the Atlantic as it splinters over hidden rocks in a headlong dash to the southern and western shores. The peninsula contains many historical relics too: Bushman artefacts, monuments to Portuguese mariners, and the remains of a wartime radar station which desecrates the summit of Vasco Dagamapiek at the southern end of the path.

The walk starts at the southern edge of the lay-by, high above Smitswinkelbaai (Blacksmith's Bay), a good spot to look at the scenery before starting out. A notice at the entrance to the path tells you that the journey to Cape Point is likely to take six hours, but this allows plenty of time for a picnic lunch as well as some swimming and sightseeing. It's not a walk to be rushed.

The path is easy to follow as it meanders towards a trio of peaks ahead, towering over the western shore of False Bay: Judas Peak, Die Boer and Paulsberg. (There are one or two short paths to cliff-edge viewpoints as the path skirts these first three peaks. All three peaks plunge precipitously into the bay, a feature which remains largely hidden if you stick to the main path.) The path climbs most of the way up Judas before crossing its western flank and clambering over the top of Die Boer. From there it drops down again and skirts the western slopes of Paulsberg before climbing to the summit of Kanonkop, where a 200-year-old cannon points out to sea — still waiting for Napoleon (**1h30min**).

Keep to the left at the cannon and follow the winding path down a picturesque gully leading to the beach north of Bordjiesdrif. An old limestone kiln marks the spot where the path descends to the road by the beach, the ground between the two often carpeted with flowers. Follow the road to the right for a short distance, before turning off left in front of a wooden WC. (Note that a sign at the beginning of this path warns picnickers not to use it. This does not apply to hikers: a right of way exists all the way along the coast.)

The grassy path eventually gives way to a car park and a brick WC on the right. Just beyond the WC the path goes past a tidal swimming pool and a *braai* (barbecue) area (**2h05min**). Higher up to the right there is a white build-

Coastal landscape on the approach to Cape Point

ing which looks from a distance like a lighthouse. On closer inspection it turns out to be a monument to various Portuguese seafarers who were unfortunate enough to fall foul of the many pirates who plied their trade in these waters during the 16th and 17th centuries. *(Note that this area is called Bordjiesdrif, one of the points where you could start or end the Shorter walks.)*

The road beyond the car park veers right, and the path also veers right a bit further on — just before reaching a small building which serves as an environment centre. It then curves to the left past another building on the left (with a notice outside it prohibiting entry) and descends to the beach, a curving sandy bay called Buffelsbaai (Buffalo Bay). After crossing the beach, the path rises to another grassy section, with a tidal pool on the left and a cross on the right (**2h20min**). The cross was erected to commemorate the 500th anniversary of Bartholomew Dias's first voyage round the Cape in 1488. Beyond the monument the path goes down to the beach once more and follows the shore to an area of low-lying rock with fine views. Apart from the huge prospect across False Bay, you can see the coastline curving back towards Paulsberg, the nearest of three peaks close to the shore. The contrast between the jagged cliffs overlooking the sea on the eastern faces of Paulsberg and Judas Peak and the benign western slopes traversed at the beginning of the walk is typical of many of the peaks along the Cape Peninsula coastline, where the sea is constantly pitting its strength against the rock.

The path now crosses a mixture of rock, sand and flowering greenery, including scarlet vygies and yellow sour figs nestling in a tangle of succulent leaves in the sand. This is where the cormorants come to fish as well; the birds can be seen perched on tall rocks at the water's edge — too sleek and fat to cause Caesar any sleepless nights, but too fast for the unwary fish.

After joining the end of a tarred road for a short distance (*the second point where a car can be left for the Shorter walks*), the path forks right about 40m/yds further on and follows the coastline — until the cliffs come straight down to the sea. The path avoids this obstacle by staggering up to the right before the cliff gets too steep (note the tiny yellow footprints painted on the rock at your feet). It's an interesting climb at the outset; the path passes two view-points soon after leaving the shore. The first, a natural plat-form of sandstone rock just off to the left, overlooks two huge tidal caves gaping seawards from the face of the cliff, the nearer one built like a sculptured tunnel, red-grained and high-arched. Further up, after the path has dallied with the edge of the cliff for a while, it reaches a walled vantage point neatly built above a plaque describing the habits and appearance of southern right and humpback whales. The former can be seen close to the shore from August to October, when they come into shallow waters to breed — a season which coincides with the spring flowers.

From here the path continues climbing the rock, before crossing another car park (**3h15min**). On the far side of the car park the narrow but clear sandy path disappears into thick bush (take the right-hand path; the path on the left goes down to the shore). Carry on climbing steadily towards the point once more, soon crossing a tarred road. It is on this section that the western coastline comes into sight for the first time, as the peninsula narrows down to little more than a kilometre in width.

On the far side of the road the path steepens con-siderably and slowly winds its way up the western flank of Vasco Dagamapiek, a rocky hill some 266m/872ft high. At its highest point (**3h40min**) the path almost reaches the summit. But there is no point in climbing to the top: not only is the old, battered wire fence to the left of the path designed to keep walkers out, but the hilltop is littered with the concrete debris of a wartime radar station. Keep to the path instead; it veers right after rounding the summit and then descends the sloping ridge to the car park below Cape Point, where the walk ends (**4h**). Many locals believe that they're looking at two oceans here — the Indian and the Atlantic ... despite the fact that the map shows the Atlantic continuing all the way to Cape Agulhas some 160km/100mi away to the southeast. It's a romantic (and profit-able) idea that flourishes regardless of the evidence — to the considerable, but so far fruitless, annoyance of the Cape Agulhas community.

15 DEVIL'S PEAK VIA MOWBRAY RIDGE

Distance/time: 12km/7.4mi; 5h30min

Grade: strenuous, with some rock-scrambling and exposure; you must be sure-footed and have a head for heights. *The walk should not be attempted in wet or windy weather.* Climb 920m/3020ft.

Equipment: walking boots, sunhat, jersey, waterproofs, picnic, plenty of water all the year round (the streams along the route are often dry); long-sleeved shirt and suncream in sunny weather

How to get there and return: 🚌 to/from the Rhodes Memorial (see Car tour 2, page 15, and the top right-hand (northeastern) corner of the walking map inside the back cover). Or on foot: this involves a short cut through the university campus, which is a feasible proposition when escorted by a member of the university, but not otherwise.

Short walk: Rhodes Memorial — Plumpudding Hill — chestnut grove — Rhodes Memorial. 4.5km/2.8mi; 1h15min. Easy. Access and equipment as main walk, but stout shoes will suffice. This is a circular walk which may be done in either direction, with a good view of the city for much of the way. Follow the main walk to the first jeep track (04min) and turn right along it, on the northeastern slope of Devil's Peak. When you come to a fork (21min), from where the ruins of the Queen's Blockhouse can be seen directly in front of you, turn left uphill. Keep climbing until the track levels out at Plumpudding Hill — marked by a beacon to the left (37min). The track now traverses the mountainside in a southerly direction. On reaching a wood, it curves left downhill, descending just at the right of a deep and wide hollow. After some 300m/yds of downhill walking (1h), double-back left off the track on a path. This takes you down into the hollow, to a copse of mature chestnuts (setting for Picnic 1). From there the path travels northwards again, leaving the wood and widening into a stony jeep track which takes you back to the memorial (1h15min).

Alternative walk: Rhodes Memorial — Lower Traverse to Oppelskop — Middle Traverse back to Rhodes Memorial. 10km/6.2mi; 3h. Moderate-energetic. Equipment and access as main walk. Climb 430m/1400ft. Follow the main walk up to the King's Blockhouse and bear right along the dwarf retaining wall (40min). Then continue straight ahead instead of turning left for Mowbray Ridge. You're now on the Lower Traverse: follow it until it dips down to a junction of paths just above the Tafelbergweg (1h). Continue straight ahead and follow the path as it climbs steadily up a series of zigzags towards Oppelskop. As the gradient eases after about 15min of climbing, turn left off the traverse on another path and start zigzagging upwards again. Another 10min of walking brings you to the ridge leading down to Oppelskop: take the narrow path leading down the ridge to the *kop* (1h30min; setting for Picnic 5a). Walk back along the ridge and then uphill to the left, towards the Middle Traverse, where you keep left. At the next junction (1h50min), climb up to the right. Continue, keeping left where a path forks off to the right near the end of the traverse. This traverse ends at Mowbray Ridge (2h15min). Descend the ridge to the King's Blockhouse and return to the memorial by your outward path.

Devil's Peak, or 'Duivelsberg' as the early Dutch settlers named it, is a near-neighbour of Table Mountain, on the southeastern outskirts of Cape Town. Occupying a dominant position in the western skyline above the city's southern suburbs, it is a high and imperious pile of earth and rock, reaching towards the sky quickly on all sides, its upper slopes shaped like an enormous sliced cone. Joined to its more renowned neighbour by a high sandstone saddle jutting out from the eastern corner of Table Mountain's northern wall, the peak (1000m/3300ft) is supported by a formidable array of rocky buttresses and ridges.

The easiest approach to the top is from the southwest — all the way up the broad slope from the saddle (the cut face of the cone), but there are several more interesting ways of achieving the summit, including the ascent described here. It climbs most of the way up the northeastern corner of the mountain: Mowbray Ridge. The route then traverses to the right and joins the southern face near the top. Mowbray Ridge is an important feature of the area, incidentally; it reaches out some distance between Cape Town and its southern suburbs, marking the border between the relatively dry northern slopes of the two mountains and their rain-drenched eastern slopes.

The path starts from the upper right-hand side of the car park next to the Rhodes Memorial, at a point some 160m/525ft above sea level (there is a small transmission substation on your right as you set out). The path is wide and steep at first, trampled into submission by thousands of heavy boots. It soon reaches a jeep track traversing the mountainside (**04min**). *(The Short walk turns right on this track.)* The path crosses the track obliquely to the left and climbs steadily across the slope before gradually levelling off. A few metres after passing a fork off to the right, the main path itself swings right, just before reaching some gaunt old pines. The path continues uphill for about 300m/yds, crosses another jeep track, and then climbs more steeply. It then bends right again and eventually reaches the wide Contour Path, which is travelling in the same direction (**30min**).

Join the Contour Path (followed in Walk 1); it takes you almost immediately to a jeep track at a hairpin bend (beyond a turnstile). Now follow the track as it curls uphill to the left — to a round pile of stonework flanked by two cannons pointing towards the northeastern hinterland (**38min**). The cannons were placed here in 1795, shortly after the first British occupation of the Cape. From here a bird's-eye view of the city can be seen, along with Table Bay, Robben Island and the Atlantic beyond. Standing between the city and the ocean are Signal Hill and Lion's Head, the two forming the rump, back and head of what to all the world looks like a seated lion. In the foreground — behind and above the cannons — stands a blockhouse, one of three forming a triangular defensive formation built soon after the occupation in 1795, against a possible invasion by the French. This is the King's Blockhouse; it stands in a conspicuous position some 480m/1575ft above the sea, just underneath a formidable-looking cliff: Mowbray Ridge. (The other two blockhouses, further down the mountainside, are in ruins).

The path now turns its back on both cannons and jeep track and climbs towards the King's Blockhouse. It rises in a westerly direction past the building's sightless northern wall and proceeds along a paved ledge between two dwarf stone retaining walls (**40min**). It then climbs through a small wood and crosses another path at a junction staggered to the left *(the Lower Traverse, where the Alternative walk keeps right).* Soon afterwards it climbs past a cylindrical concrete water tank and makes for the cliff-face. From now on the boot prints are few and far-between.

After zigzagging upwards for a short distance, the path traverses to the right along the northern face of the cliff, gradually rising at first and then scrambling up some easy rock, just before switching back to the east. It then goes through the whole procedure again, in reverse. There is a brief moment of exposure as it switches direction for the second time, but apart from that the path is secure, its surface solid rock.

The route now zigzags steeply uphill in a southwesterly direction, passing two level paths going off to the right. *(The first is the Middle Traverse, where the Alternative walk rejoins the main route;* the second is another path leading down to the Middle Traverse.) You climb to a firewatcher's hut (**1h10min**) secured to a rocky promontory 600m/1970ft above sea level. You're now about halfway to the top of Devil's Peak from the car park.

From the hut the path becomes much easier again, continuing its southwesterly ascent, but on a more gradual slope. As it climbs higher, the ridge widens into a kind of rough meadow, scattered with heather, daisies, irises and lilies — as thick as thieves and just as scratchy. In the middle of all this another contour path goes off to the right: the Upper Traverse (**1h30min**). Turn right along it. *(Do **not** continue straight ahead up the ridge: the path is eroded in places and needs attention. It is also very exposed at some points. In fact it is risky at all times and should not be attempted without a guide, regardless of its condition.)*

The traverse on the other hand is superb, one of the best anywhere on the mountain, opening out a series of wide uninterrupted prospects to the north and east and even-

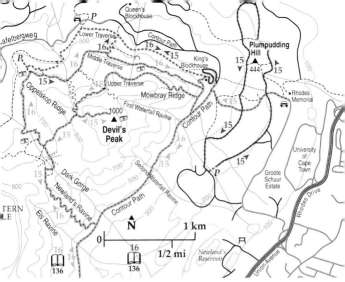

tually to the south, to the towering northern wall of Table Mountain. The path has its own atmosphere too: aloof from its distant surroundings, it meanders in a southwesterly direction along the mountain's high sloping face, occasionally passing over a cliff or buttress, at one point under an overhanging rock, and several times in and out of running streams. If you're lucky you might see a pair of black eagles on this traverse; their territory covers both Devil's Peak and Table Mountain. They are magnificent birds — remarkable fliers with huge black and white wings that seldom move as they glide over the mountain, changing pace and direction apparently without effort — masters of all they survey.

The traverse crosses a path coming down from the saddle to the left after about **1h53min** and then continues in a more dishevelled state on the far side. It contours through thick bush to another overgrown path zigzagging upwards again, which soon clears the bush and emerges on a shoulder on the southwestern face of Devil's Peak — the cut face of the cone (**2h20min**). From here a good path wriggles up to the summit, the topmost point being marked by the second of three survey beacons (**2h45min**). There's little to get in the way of the view from up here, a 360° panorama: the huge northeastern wall of Table Mountain, Lion's Head, Signal Hill, the ocean, Table Bay to the north and False Bay to the southeast, the distant mountains and the sprawling conurbation of greater Cape Town, its marshalling yards and harbour now far enough away to look like models of the real thing.

Once you've had your fill of the scenery, return by the

same path until it reaches the shoulder again. Then, instead of descending the zigzags of your upward path, continue straight down to the saddle between Devil's Peak and Table Mountain (**3h30min**). Turn left at a four-way junction on the saddle and then, after passing two fire-break paths coming down from the left, go right. There is a notice at this turning, with an arrow pointing right (with a little imagination, you can pick out the words 'Newlands Ravine' on it.) Do **not** go straight ahead at this point, as the path ahead leads to Dark Gorge — a dangerous descent.

Follow the new path upwards until it reaches another obscure signpost indicating Newlands Ravine. It is not at all clear which way this leaning sign is pointing, but that doesn't matter: the path going straight ahead and the other one going left both lead uphill to the top of Newlands Ravine — where another weathered signpost points the way down (**3h55min**). Walk down the ravine; it is very steep and rocky in places, but a good path zigzags down its centre. After a descent of about 400m/1300ft you arrive at the Contour Path at the bottom of the ravine (**4h45min**). Turn left and follow the Contour Path back to the turnstile above the Rhodes Memorial. Then follow your outgoing path back to your car (**5h30min**).

Devil's Peak from the road to the Rhodes Memorial

16 A CIRCULAR WALK ROUND DEVIL'S PEAK

See map inside the back cover to begin and end the walk; see map page 93 for the circuit round Devil's Peak

Distance/time: 15km/9.3mi; 4h45min

Grade: strenuous on the ascent of Newlands Ravine, otherwise relatively easy. You must be sure-footed. Climb 700m/2300ft.

Equipment: walking boots or stout shoes, sunhat, jersey, waterproofs, picnic, water; long-sleeved shirt and suncream in sunny weather

How to get there and return: 🚌 See *Short walk 2* on page 38, to park in the lay-by on the forest side of Union Avenue.

Short walk: The Woodcutter's Trail: 3km/2mi; 1h15min. *See map on the reverse of the touring map, inside the back cover.* Easy. Wear walking boots or stout shoes. Access: Drive along Union Avenue until you come to the Newlands Forestry Station on the left (about 0.7km from the traffic lights). Take the road to the right as you drive in, and park under the trees on the left. Walk over to the left and join the road leading through the Forestry Station towards the mountain. When you reach a T-junction, turn left (note the helicopter pad on the right). After a few hundred metres/yards, turn right and follow a path on the right-hand bank of a wide stream. It soon reaches a broad path which you follow to the right for about ten paces, before picking up the upstream path again. Cross a jeep track (15min) and continue alongside the stream until you come to another path forking left (22min): cross the stream here. The path now rises for five minutes before bending right and recrossing the stream. An easy traverse takes you to a jeep track (43min), where you turn right and head downhill. The track turns sharp left and descends to a T-junction (1h). Turn right on this track but, after only a few paces, take a broad path down to the left. This path drops down to another jeep track, where you turn right downhill. On coming to a fork just after a crossing track, turn left. About 300m/yds further on, take a path down to the right — back to the helicopter pad. Walk back to the car park from there.

This walk climbs through Newlands Forest to the Contour Path, then up Newlands Ravine and round Devil's Peak in a clockwise direction, before returning through the forest. The route is a delight, the terrain constantly changing: forest, ravine, high saddle, buttresses and spectacular traverses — there is something to please the eye all the way round. The walk is a little longer than Walk 15 but is less arduous — and a little less remote from terra firma. But bear in mind that Devil's Peak was once called Windberg, a name which is equally apt today. Choose a calm day before setting out: if the 'tablecloth' on Table Mountain is swirling about, find somewhere else to walk: the upper section of Newlands Ravine is very unpleasant in a southeaster.

To start out, climb up the embankment by the lay-by on to a pavement and walk uphill for about 300m/yds, then take a footpath turning left into the trees. After passing through a gap in a fence, it continues to an open area next to a jeep track (**11min**). There is a walkers' map here, on the far side of the track. Turn left up the jeep track and then go right on another track. Turn left after a few hundred paces, taking a wide path which climbs through pines to a third jeep track. Turn right along the track and then go left at a junction soon afterwards. Follow the winding track until it doubles back left by a clearing. Take the path to the right at the end of the hairpin bend — heading for a signpost pointing to the Contour Path. Follow the path uphill through indigenous woodland until it emerges on the jeep track again. Turn right on the jeep track and follow it for about 100 paces, to its end. Then take a path up to the left and join the Contour Path (at an acute angle). Keep walking in the same direction along the Contour Path until, soon after crossing heavy scree, you arrive at the foot of Newlands Ravine (**50min**), where there is a makeshift sign at the foot of the path. From here refer to the map on page 93.

Except for the first section of the climb, which concentrates on contouring back above the scree, this ravine is very steep — one of the steepest on the mountain. Its upper reaches are hemmed in by vertical cliffs to the right and a high ridge to the left. The zigzag path at its centre is well made, but there is no escaping the steepness of the climb ahead. On the way up you may catch sight of some strange shaggy creatures on the cliffs bordering the ravine. They are *tahrs* — Himalayan mountain goats, released from a zoo in Rondebosch a few years ago, when it closed. This decision has proved controversial, as the goats do not have the same instinctive respect for their surroundings as the mountain's natural inhabitants. As well as being agile, they are prolific, so it is not easy to keep their numbers down.

Once you've clambered to the top (**1h45min**), follow the path straight ahead. It curves right after a while and then forks right, before descending to the saddle below Devil's Peak — the latter sloping steeply upwards to the northeast. Turn left by a signpost and cross three paths, the first two being fire-breaks and the third a genuine path leading up to the summit of Devil's Peak on the right. Your path veers left beyond this third path and soon arrives at a T-junction by a large rock (**2h05min**). There is an excellent view of both town and mountain from here, as well as extensive views across the ocean and the land to the north.

At this point a path leads left down to the Tafelbergweg which traverses across the northern face of Table Mountain to Kloofnek. The path to the right is the Middle Traverse round Devil's Peak — the route you now follow: it zigzags downhill at first and then rounds a rocky buttress to the right. This is a spectacular part of the walk, on a remarkably well-designed path which somehow manages to cross the

Oppelskop (Picnic 5a) from Devil's Peak

steep terrain without undue exposure. As the path finally clears the buttress, Oppelskop Ridge comes into view. The path carries on above the ridge and then traverses all the way back to Mowbray Ridge . There is just one tricky point along the traverse: about 10 minutes past the *second* path down to Oppelskop, look out for a path going up to the right — this is your path, *not* the more obvious one going straight ahead.* Your path levels out after a short climb and then descends once more. You pass a path going up right to the fire-watcher's hut, and shortly thereafter arrive at Mowbray Ridge (**3h05min**).

The view from Mowbray Ridge is almost as good as the one from the top of Devil's Peak, but your descent to the King's Blockhouse does not mix with sightseeing. *The path requires your undivided attention;* it descends very steeply — sometimes precipitously — down the rocky cliff which marks the bottom of Mowbray Ridge. From the cannons below the blockhouse (see notes page 91), follow a jeep track curling down to a turnstile on the Contour Path (**3h35min**). Walk through the turnstile and along the Contour Path to the bottom of Newlands Ravine, a journey of about 2km/1.2mi through thick forest. Then retrace your steps to Union Avenue (**4h45min**).

*But you may *prefer* to take the path straight ahead in order to avoid Mowbray Ridge, which is exposed in places and tricky in a strong wind. The path straight ahead soon starts to descend and branches out into three lower paths — one zigzagging down to the Lower Traverse and the other two petering out between the two traverses. The Lower Traverse undulates back to the King's Blockhouse after almost descending to the Tafelbergweg. This option takes about the same time as continuing on the Middle Traverse and down Mowbray Ridge.

17 LION'S HEAD

See also cover photograph   **Distance/time**: 4km/2.5mi; about 2h

Grade: strenuous, particularly near the summit where there is some scrambling over rock. *Possibility of vertigo*. Climb 380m/1250ft.

Equipment: walking boots (preferable) or stout shoes, jersey, waterproofs, sunhat, (optional) picnic, water; long-sleeved shirt and suncream in sunny weather. Note that there is *no water* on the mountain.

How to get there and return: 🚐 Follow Car tour 2 (page 16) to Kloofnek, then turn right towards Signal Hill and park in a lay-by on the right about 600m up the road. Another starting point is at a car park up on the left about 1.5km from the *nek*, but the main walk starts from the lay-by. There are walkers' maps at both these starting points.

Alternative walks:

1   Circuit round Lion's Head from Kloofnek. 5km/3mi; 1h30min. Easy. Climb 100m/330ft. Equipment as main walk. Access: park in the car park to the left of the roundabout at Kloofnek. Walk across the roundabout and then down the road to the left of Signal Hill (Kloof Road). After about 7min of downhill walking, a path goes uphill to the right. Follow this path as it rises and then circumnavigates the mountain in a clockwise direction. The path descends to another path coming in from the left and then forks twice as it travels along the western slopes of Lion's Head: keep right both times. In due course the path rises to a T-junction (1h05min), where you turn right and climb to a car park 1.5km from Kloofnek. From there walk down Signal Hill Road and back to the car.

2   Circuit round Signal Hill. 6km/3.7mi; 1h55min. Moderate. Climb 150m/500ft. Equipment as main walk. Access: park at the car park to the left of Signal Hill Road, about 1.5km from Kloofnek. Take the path down to the left from the southern end of the car park and follow it all the way along the western flank of Signal Hill. When it it swings to the right and comes to a fork (30min), climb up to the right. The path winds upwards at the edge of a gum plantation and then traverses left to a gully, where you ignore a path rising to the right. Keep traversing left and make your way past a series of dug-outs; the path continues on the far side. A little later (55min), a jeep track comes in from the left and the path forks right. Leave the path here: follow the track until it arrives at a gate. Climb to the right here, alongside a security fence surrounding the Signal Hill Battery (where an artillery piece fires a noonday signal every day of the year). Then, when the fence turns steeply downhill, take a jeep track off to the right. Climb to a T-junction and turn right, to ascend to the top of Signal Hill. You cross the tarred road near the summit, which is reached in 1h25min. From here follow a footpath leading from the picnic area along the spine of Signal Hill towards Lion's Head, until you reach the car park.

Lion's Head is one of the most conspicuous landmarks in Cape Town. Smaller, but no less dramatic than Table Mountain itself, the peak forms the highest point of a long hill (Signal Hill) shaped like a seated lion, the head at the southern end 669m/2194ft high and the rump, a couple of kilometres to the north, 350m/1148ft high. The hill's nearest northern equivalent must be Edinburgh's Arthur's Seat, but the head adds an extra dimension: a spectacular steeple of bare rock — a magnet that attracts and repels at the same time, a climb to tackle once you've 'got your eye in' on Table Mountain.

It is obvious, looking at the head, that there must be some degree of exposure towards the summit, and there is. But the path's architect has smoothed the perilous ruffles with such skill that most people will be able to climb to the top and down again with a fair degree of assurance. In fact, the locals sometimes go up in the evening and come down again by the light of a full moon, after watching the sun sink into the ocean — a memorable experience for those who know the way. But whatever the time of day, the view from the top is hard to beat.

To start the walk, cross the road from the lay-by and

walk up the jeep track on the far side. The route spirals up the peak like a corkscrew, starting on the eastern side and finishing on the southern corner, having completed a circle and a quarter from its starting point. Early on, the jeep track narrows into a rough path as it swings gradually round the mountain in a clockwise direction. After about **30min** a path goes off left — which links with the car park on the northern side of Lion's Head. Continue circling the mountain until a signpost points up to the right (**36min**). (The path straight ahead is more difficult and best avoided.)

The right-hand path now steepens as it engages the mountain more intimately, beginning a traverse across the northern and eastern flanks of the peak — helped at one point by a ladder. Keep walking along the eastern flank, past another signpost pointing straight on, and then climb the southern corner. This route is a little exposed at times and entails a fair amount of scrambling, but it avoids the chains on the route that climbs to the right at the previous signpost. There is a second ladder to climb near the summit, which is reached in about **1h10min**.

The summit has been landscaped to minimise erosion and is small enough to make a score of people a crowd. There is a superb view in all directions, especially the one of Table Mountain's northwestern corner (Kloof Corner) and the Twelve Apostles beyond it to the right. You also get a very good view of the mountains in the distant hinterland, as well as the western coastline and the city sprawled below.

You have two options for the descent (aside from the chains). The first is the simple one of re-tracing your steps, which takes about 50 minutes, or **2h** in all. The second involves turning right soon after dropping onto the traverse along the western flank (by the first signpost, about 30 minutes from the summit — and note that you take the *second* turning down to the right, not the first which is too eroded to descend safely). This path takes you down to the car park which lies on the Lion's back in another 20 minutes. From there the walk down to the lay-by takes about 12 minutes (**2h12min**).

Top: Cape Town from Signal Hill. Middle: flowering gum tree on the road from Kloofnek to Signal Hill. Bottom: Table Mountain from high up on the eastern face of Lion's Head.

18 THE ALPHEN TRAIL

Distance/time: 7km/4.3mi; 2h

Grade: easy: a woodland trail, easy underfoot, with gentle gradients. Note that the paths double as bridle paths, horses having the right of way.

Equipment: comfortable walking shoes, sunhat, (optional) picnic, water; suncream and a long-sleeved shirt in sunny weather. The Alphen Hotel, where the walk starts and ends, provides lunches and teas.

How to get there and return: 🚗 From Rondebosch drive along Newlands Avenue to the traffic lights at Union Avenue, then turn left on Paradise Road. Keep going along the dual carriageway (M3) until you arrive at the Constantia junction (M41), where you turn off left. Turn left at the end of the slip road and right at the next set of traffic lights. Park at the side of the road 150m from the lights: this is where the path goes off left.

Short walks: Follow either branch of the Dieprivier and return the same way (1h30min), or walk up the Dieprivier on one bank and return on the other: there are three bridges where one can cross (30min). Alternatively, park for Picnic 3 at Bel Ombre (see Car tour 1, page 11), and use the map to walk as far as you like from there.

A change from mountain walking, this ramble alongside the Dieprivier and several of its tributaries penetrates pockets of green countryside stretching down from Table Mountain into the heart of Constantia, one of Cape Town's loveliest suburbs. It is quite unlike any other walk in the book: a quiet saunter through green meadows lined with leafy trees, the mountains rising in the distance rather than directly above your head. *Don't* be put off by the 'urban'-looking roads on the map: the entire walk meanders through a green belt — you'll hardly see a house all day.

The route is shaped like a catapult, the handle following the left or southern bank of the Dieprivier, whose source lies above Bel Ombre on Table Mountain. The right-hand limb runs alongside the Klaasenbosch Stream which flows down the Cecilia and Spilhouse ravines before joining the Diep at the catapult's crotch. The left-hand limb follows the Dieprivier itself. The 'sling' is formed by a path through Cecilia Forest — my suggested extension to the route

shown on the trail maps posted alongside the path at various strategic points along the way.

To start the walk, follow the path past a notice board welcoming you to the Alphen Trail and displaying a large trail map. The Dieprivier is on your right, another path skirting its far bank. After some **17min** of walking the trail forks: turn right over a wooden bridge and continue on the far side, branching right a couple of times before descending to Hohenhort Avenue (**25min**). (All the paths beyond the bridge descend to Hohenhort Avenue: keeping right cuts a few corners.)

Walk down the road to the right for about two hundred paces, then cross the road and join the path once more (by another trail map). Bear left soon after rejoining the path, which now enters thick woodland and wanders along the northern bank of the Klaasenbosch. The path turns left across the stream after a while and then heads right at a junction (where another path veers left to Hohenhort Avenue). A succession of high garden fences now borders the path on the left as it continues along the southern bank of the stream, before recrossing it and climbing to Spilhaus Avenue (**45min**).

Turn left and walk along the road for about two hundred paces, then turn right into Hohenhort Avenue once more. The avenue rises to Rhodes Drive opposite the Cecilia Forest car park. Cross the road, walk through the car park, and follow the jeep track on the far side (**55min**). The track rises steadily through pines to a T-junction: keep left here, continuing gently uphill through the plantation.

Left: Oak trees at Bel Ombre (Picnic 3) display their brilliant colours like golden peacocks. Right: from the 'crotch of the catapult' there are fine views to the eastern flank of Table Mountain's Back Table, with Constantia Corner sloping down to the left and Cecilia Ravine at the centre.

About 10 minutes beyond the car park, a path leads down to the left through the trees — the first of three that descend to Rhodes Drive after traversing above it for some distance. Take one of these paths (if they are not blocked by tree-felling), or keep to the track — it eventually descends left and reaches the road at the same point as the paths (**1h15min**). The paths are more scenic; the first one goes through a grove of cork oaks as it nears the road.

Cross Rhodes Drive and walk down Southern Cross Drive on the far side, to another Alphen Trail signpost. At this point the route heads left to follow the other limb of the catapult, beginning its downhill journey back to the fork at the bridge. The path soon crosses two more roads (Bellevue Avenue and Monterey Drive) and then runs down to the left of Bel Ombre Drive, before crossing it and arriving at a junction of two paths in a grassy clearing surrounded by trees (**1h25min**), the setting for Picnic 3. This is a lovely place to take a break. The trees are a fine sight at any time of the year but, on an autumn day, when the slanting sun casts its soft light on the richly-coloured leaves, all else fades into oblivion. There are some very fine oaks in this grove. The Cape winter is too short and warm for European oaks; rot sets in early. As a result, the wood is not hard enough for the nearby vineyards, which use imported oak for the barrels that mature their wine and brandy.

Take the path down to the left from the junction (the other path goes straight ahead to Klaasenbosch Drive). From here the way is clear; the path meanders through thick woodland once more, before crossing a bridge across a marsh and coming into an open meadow. After a gentle descent through the meadow, the path crosses Brommersvlei Road at another signpost and map, then gradually closes on the Dieprivier which lies hidden in thick reeds over to the left. The path then rejoins the outer route at the bridge and wends its way back to the starting point (**2h**).

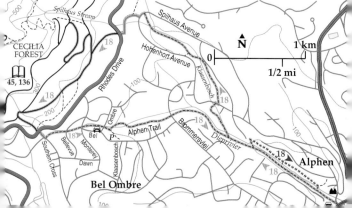

9 HELDERBERG: WESTERN PEAK

Distance/time: 12km/
7.4mi; 4h35min

Grade: strenuous.
Climb 880m/2885ft.

Equipment: walking
boots, jersey, water-
proofs, sunhat, pic-
nic, water; suncream
and long-sleeved shirt
in sunny weather.
*There is only one
waterhole en route.*

**How to get there and
return**: 🚌 to/from the
Helderberg   Nature
Reserve,   on   the
northern outskirts of
Somerset West. Take
the N2 motorway
from Cape Town and
turn off at the Strand
exit about 40km to
the east. Turn left
again at the top of the
slip road and right at
the traffic lights about
2km uphill. The re-
serve is signposted to
the left at the third set
of traffic lights along
this road (an extra
lane allowing you to
filter left). About 2km
along, turn left at a
crossroad with a Shell
garage just beyond it,
then go right two
junctions further on
and left at the next
junction. The gates of
the reserve soon ap-
pear, beyond a left-

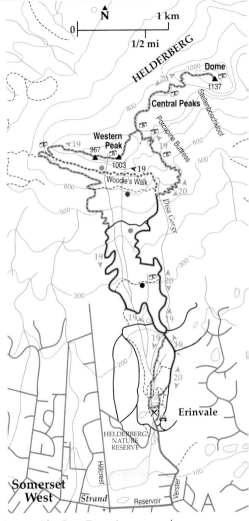

hand bend. (Take the *Street guide: Cape Town,* in case you lose your
way: it includes both Somerset West and Stellenbosch).

Short walks: There are many walks within the gardens (Picnic 12),
designed to show off the shrubs, trees and flowers. Follow whichever path
takes your fancy. The Inner Reserve is smaller than Kirstenbosch and less
manicured, but there is a wide variety of proteas and an abundance of bird
life — including Cape sugar-birds and orange-breasted sunbirds. There
are lily ponds too, and a larger pond behind the thatch-roofed restaurant,
where a variety of waterbirds have made their homes.

Alternative walks: The main entrance to the gardens is through an
archway to the left of the car park. Just inside the archway, under glass, is
a map illustrating several colour-coded walks: yellow, black, blue, red

105

and green; the yellow one is the shortest and the green one (Woodie's Walk) the longest — about 10km/6mi. They all meander around on the southern slopes of the mountain in the Outer Reserve, using a mixture of jeep tracks and paths. They're also well-enough signposted to follow without a description (see coloured circles on the map), easy to moderate in grade, and can be tackled in walking shoes. The one exception is Woodie's Walk, which is particularly beautiful in spring:

Woodie's Walk. 10km/6.2mi; 3h40min. Moderate-strenuous. Climb 600m/1970ft. Equipment and access as main walk. Follow the main walk to Disa Gorge (1h05min). Then continue up the gorge past the red route (marked with an arrow). The path now climbs steeply to the left of the rock-strewn bed of the gorge, eventually arriving at a green arrow where you turn left and leave the Disa. The path continues climbing as it clears the trees lining the gorge and then traverses west underneath the southern face of the Western Peak. *Watch the path through two minor gorges on the traverse carefully: both times the path drops into the gorge and rises out again. It is easy to continue downhill and miss the path altogether.* Just before the end of the traverse, a path forks up to the right (2h05min). Follow it up to a flat rock, an outstanding viewpoint. Then continue along the traverse. From this point there is no further problem: follow the main walk downhill, picking up the notes just after the 3h-point.

Helderberg (Clear Mountain) lies between the town of Somerset West and a long range of mountains called the Hottentots-Holland, which runs northwards from the eastern shores of False Bay. There are various theories about the origin of the range's name, but the most likely one is that at one stage in Colonial history it marked the frontier of Hottentot or Khoi territory. At the point where the Helderberg joins the Hottentots-Holland range, the latter spreads out into a hand of four fingers: from north to east, the Stellenbosch, Jonkershoek, Groot-Drakenstein and Franschhoek ranges. Helderberg marches away in a westerly direction from the wrist, towards False Bay, a long ridge of eight peaks ending at the Western Peak.

The mountain's highest point, at 1137m/3729ft, is the Dome, the fifth peak from the west. Beyond the Dome, the three eastern peaks are completely wild, having no paths and no access except through private land. But the five westernmost peaks, all accessible from the gardens, are all worth the climb, the Dome (Walk 20) particularly giving very fine views all round. In this walk, however, the Western Peak takes centre stage — a mountain characterised by quietness, solitude, and an abundance of wildlife. This is the home of eagle, falcon, baboon and hare; of lizard, tortoise, orange-breasted sunbird and the ubiquitous red-winged starling. A myriad of plants grows on its slopes, below the tall cliffs on its southern face — and higher up on the other faces, mingling with the rocks that climb to its lofty summit, over 1000m/3300ft above the sea.

The walk starts from the top right-hand corner of the reserve's car park. Walk off to the right along the edge of a grassy embankment and then go left after a few paces, where three well-worn paths branch out. Take the middle path, overlooking a series of lily-ponds in a deep hollow on the left. Once past the ponds, climb uphill to the right on a steep path. When you emerge on a jeep track running uphill towards the mountain, follow it due north, with the gardens on the left and the Hottentots-Holland range on the right. The Western Peak is directly in front of you.

After about 1km/0.6mi of easy walking, the track passes through a small gate in a high fence separating the Inner and Outer Reserves. (Keep left at the fork in the track about 250m/yds *before* the gate.) Immediately after the gate there is a second fork. Both tracks lead towards the top, but the route to the right is steeper and easier to climb up than down, so take the right-hand track and keep the left-hand one for your return. The track steepens immediately after the junction and then winds uphill through banks of thick *fynbos*. After a few twists and turns the track climbs sharply and arrives at a junction, where a route waymarked in black goes off left along a contour path. A wooden bench looks out to sea at this point, and across to the mountains beyond the town. The track now winds its way upwards once more — until it arrives at another junction where a blue-marked route continues to the left.

Turn right at this point (following the direction of a flotilla of arrows) and walk up the track to its end, a few hundred metres/yards further on (**1h05min**). The track ends at Disa Gorge, a steep and thickly-wooded ravine separating the Western Peak from Porcupine Buttress to the east — your route to the top. Up until now the Disa Stream has

View over the Helderberg valley vineyards to the Hottentots-Holland range from Porcupine Buttress. 'Spy-glass Hill' is to the far right.

been falling further and further below you to the right, but at this point the path and stream come together. This stream, incidentally, is the only perennial source of water on the whole trip.

Now a path continues up the gorge, at the left of the stream, through a jungle of exposed tree roots. After about a hundred paces, on the far bank, the ground widens out a little. A signpost stands to the left of the path, with a pink arrow pointing your way across the stream (by a large rock leaning towards the mountain). The path crosses the stream just above the rock and climbs out of the trees into thick *fynbos* once more, beginning an easterly zigzag traverse across open mountainside. *(But the red route and Woodie's Walk continue straight up the gorge here.)*

After six-and-a-half zigzags, the path switches to the left and begins climbing Porcupine Buttress, twisting upwards to a rocky platform high up on its southern face — about 700m/2300ft above sea level. This is a good place to rest, for the way is steep and the rock has an unimpeded view of the mountainside below and the country beyond. Further away to the south are the rolling hills and vineyards of the Helderberg valley, with the Kogelberge in the background. To the left, as you look southwards, stands the main wall of the Hottentots-Holland Ridge, climbing north to Somerset-Sneeukop (Somerset Snow-Hill), the ridge's highest point at 1590m/5217ft. Further south on the same ridge is Verkykerskop (Spy-glass Hill), topped by its modern equivalent, a microwave tower! Over to the right, to the southwest, is False Bay, with Somerset West and its coastal neighbour, Strand — the latter's dazzling high-rise buildings partly obscuring the bay's northern shore.

Soon after leaving the rock, the path climbs to a wide shoulder sloping gradually down to the right. The Central Peaks, between the Western Peak and the Dome, have been hidden for a while by the lower reaches of Porcupine Buttress. This shoulder reintroduces them — in a truly remarkable fashion. As the view behind you becomes restricted by the ridge, a totally new one replaces it in front — a sight that never ceases to amaze me, no matter how many times I climb up here. Only a few hundred metres ahead stands the mountain's innermost sanctuary, silent as a medieval castle. Outer ramparts breached, the citadel's inner walls rise sheer to the sky: ageless cliffs of grey

weathered sandstone. In fact, the cliff that guards the southern approach to the third of the Central Peaks is so sheer that it looks as though it were cleft by a massive meat-axe, the shattered remnants of the severed rock lying half-hidden in the tangled bush below. Some distance to the right, at a slight angle, the huge wall supporting the Dome reaches high above the nearer peaks, the tiny summit beacon just visible to the right of a lone pine tree silhouetted above the cliff. To the left of the Central Peaks stands the summit of Porcupine Buttress, an abrupt outcrop of rock at the foot of the Western Peak — the latter's summit further left still, hidden by an intervening horizon. To cap it all, this sudden wildness is further enhanced by two reptilian creatures carved from the rock by wind and rain, on top of the cliff below the summit of the second Central Peak. Both creatures are petrified in attitudes of animated communication, the one below craning its neck upwards in a timeless attempt to hear the other.

The path staggers to the left from the shoulder and, keeping the view in sight the whole way, clambers up-wards to a wide ledge on the eastern face of the buttress. This ledge provides a welcome break from climbing, for it continues northwards for some distance, until it ends at a path leading up a wide ravine between the Western Peak and the Central Peaks. The ravine forms the upper reaches of a steep, wide rolling slope that climbs up the mountain-side to the foot of the inner ramparts — hidden till now by Porcupine Buttress and the shoulder at its side.

The ledge ends under an overhanging rock, where one has to jump down onto the path below. The path now zigzags slowly up the ravine until it meets a short path from Disa Gorge coming in from the left. The two combine forces and climb to a saddle lying between the Central Peaks and the Western Peak (**2h05min**). It is worth taking this section of the walk slowly, for it is a lonely part of the mountain, where much can be seen. The ravine teems with *Watsonias* (irises) in late spring and early summer, particularly after a fire, when both bulb and flower are galvanized into vigorous renewal. Red-winged starlings often fly up and down the ravine too, their melancholy cries echoing in the morning air, and Cape rock-jumpers — red-breasted birds the size of small pigeons — literally jumping from rock to rock just out of reach, as though guiding you on your way. And watch out for a large troop of baboons that regards this territory as its own: give them the right of way and they will give you a wide berth too.

From the saddle the path turns left and starts up the northern face of the Western Peak, contouring westwards at first and then climbing steeply up the rock. The path is indistinct and splits several times: there is no earth to speak of as the path rises higher, only large slabs of rock to scramble over. Keep to the left initially; then, after climbing about 70m/230ft, follow the lie of the land to the right. The path between the rocks becomes more obvious then, leading through a gap well to the right and onto a small plateau, before ascending again and emerging suddenly at the beacon on the summit (1003m/3290ft; **2h30min**).

The view from here is long and wide, embracing sea, mountain, vineyard and forest for as far as the eye can see. The whole of False Bay, the entire length of the peninsula, and the rolling country to the ocean are all laid out before you, together with the nearby mountains: the Central Peaks (at eye-level), the Dome, and the higher ridges behind it. This is black eagle country too: a pair has a nest on the mountain somewhere, for certain. Both adults and juvenile are often to be seen, sometimes separately and sometimes together, their wings catching every rising current of air.

The summit of the mountain marks the halfway point of the hike. From here the path continues its anti-clockwise route along the peak's rocky profile — a long ridge which drops down in a series of steep pitches intermixed with plateaux. You pass a lower beacon en route. After about 1km/0.6mi, the path drops down onto a natural platform at the western end of the peak, from where it descends steeply to the left. Shortly afterwards it crosses another rocky promontory, before dropping to the top (green-marked)

The Central Peaks from Porcupine Buttress (top) and pincushion proteas

contour path: Woodie's Walk (**3h**).

Double back to the right here and follow the path downhill. It swings sharply to the left and then descends gradually from west to east, the peak's southern face in shadow high up on your left. Eventually, after 1km or so, the path veers right and traverses the mountainside in the opposite direction, before curling down to the end of a jeep track — where a battered bench faces the mountain. From here the track slopes down to the southeast before joining the main route, which sweeps down the mountainside well to the west of your upward track. It passes the black-marked contour path further down and then a path down to the right, where the route waymarked in yellow meanders back to the gardens. About 0.5km/0.3mi past the yellow-marked path, the track returns to the gate to the Inner Reserve, where it rejoins your outward track.

The path back to the car park goes off right just beyond the gate, opposite a wooden bench. It takes you through the centre of the Inner Reserve, where you are likely to see proteas at their best — king proteas and pincushions among them, the flowers Cape sugar-birds feed on. They too are often to be seen, their long tails fluttering in the breeze as they fly from flower to flower, in a buzz of constant chatter. Towards the end of the journey, the path swings close to the Disa Stream again, its banks scattered with flowering trees in springtime. The end of the walk (**4h35min**) is marked by a thatched-roofed restaurant with a garden, a pond with an island in the middle (where Egyptian geese, mallards, moorhens and Cape weavers nest), and a small natural history museum, housing many examples of the area's flora, fauna and geology.

20 HELDERBERG DOME

See map page 105; see also photographs pages 107, 108-109, 111, 121

Distance 15km/9.3mi; 6h35min

Grade: very strenuous: there is a fair degree of scrambling, the terrain being extremely steep in places and rocky on top. Note too that although the walk starts at 120m, altitude is lost on the contour path, extending the climb. Climb 1100m/3610ft.

Equipment: walking boots, jersey, waterproofs, sunhat, picnic, water; suncream, long-sleeved shirt in sunny weather. There is *only one source of water* — in Disa Gorge, which you cross on the ascent and descent.

How to get there; Short and Alternative walks: see Walk 19, page 105.

The Helderberg Dome, 1137m/3732ft high, dominates the farms, forests and vineyards at its feet with a cheerful indifference. More often than not, this spectacular peak is bathed in sunlight, while the mountains forming the huge massif behind it are covered in cloud. Whether the cloud is a swirling white one formed by the dry southeast wind, or a more menacing one from the northwest, the mountain lives up to its name: clear mountain. From a distance this cheerful indifference seems to stem as much from impregnability as meteorological good fortune. The cliffs forming its southern face (the face you see from the reserve below) are among the most severe one can imagine. In fact, its summit looks totally surrounded by extremely steep sides. Moreover, as you draw closer, this impression is confirmed rather than contradicted — a disconcerting experience when tackling the mountain for the first time. However, rest assured that there *is* a path up, which contrives somehow or other to avoid the terrifying abyss one is expecting at every turn. The climb obviously requires some effort, but it is one of the most scenic in this book.

To start the hike, follow Walk 19 (page 107) as far as the Porcupine saddle (**2h05min**). Turn right instead of left at the saddle, on a winding and undulating contour path under the northern faces of the Central Peaks. This is impressive country, craggy gorges and buttresses rising and falling above and below you. After about 1km/0.6mi, the path approaches a second gorge, the one between the third of the Central Peaks and the Dome. The path begins to rise as it enters this second gorge, gently at first, but soon very steeply to the right. It climbs in and out of a rocky streambed so steeply that you'll probably need to use hand-holds. The gradient eases only a little after about 60m/200ft of climbing and then rises to a high saddle overlooking another steep gorge plunging down the southern face of the mountain. This is Stellenboschkloof, one of the loneliest and loveliest gorges you can imagine. Follow the path a little further to the left, and the *kloof* opens out at your feet. This primeval gorge looks as if it has remained untouched for millions of years. It narrows as it drops, the densely-growing trees at its centre hemmed in by jagged cliffs. To the left is the huge rock wall beneath the Dome, its true colours revealed for the very first time. As the path moves even further left you come face to face with it. However, there is no need to take a deep breath: the path turns abruptly left just before reaching the wall and begins another steep climb; leaving the rock face well alone.

After heading north for a while, the path dog-legs to the right, rising even more steeply to the southwestern end of the long ridge that forms the rocky summit of the mountain. On the climb to the ridge, the Central Peaks behind you gradually sink below your line of vision, and the Western Peak and its two beacons are revealed like features on a contour map. *Note a couple of jutting rocks as you reach the ridge, with cairns on top of them (the lower of the two looks like a wedge-shaped diving board): these are your markers on the return journey. The route along the top is not always easy to follow, particularly in cloud.*

From this point to the top (about 600m/0.4mi over to the right) takes about 15 minutes, the beacon appearing after much boulder-hopping and path-searching. (As a general guide, the path keeps to the right and centre of the ridge, rather than the left; it stays close to the top all the way.) The whole climb takes about **3h45min**. *Take careful note of the route along the spine of the ridge before you relax: despite the mountain's justified reputation for clarity, its summit has been known to disappear under cloud creeping up from below with little or no warning.*

The Western Peak (left) and the Dome (right), from the car park

The rocky summit of the Dome, with the author 'lost' in the foreground.

One of the highlights of this walk is undoubtedly the 360° view from the top, totally unimpeded by anything nearby. You will see the peninsula and Table Mountain quite easily, as well as False Bay and the distant ocean, all lying to the west and northwest. Elsewhere the mountains go on forever, too numerous to name except for one or two of the nearer ones. The high mountain standing in the foreground to the northeast is Haelkop, sitting astride the Stellenbosch Ridge; the rest of the ridge spreads out to the left. The Hottentots-Holland range stretches out to the right. You can see the dragon-like spine of Simonsberg too, over to the left, partly obscured by the Stellenbosch Ridge. Jonkershoek Ridge rises over Haelkop's left shoulder, with Victoria Peak well to the right of Haelkop, its green dome only a metre lower than the summit of Somerset-Sneeukop, the highest point of the Hottentots-Holland range. This dome lies to the left of the Triplets, which form part of the foreground to your right. Below are vineyards, orchards and plantations, watered by dozens and dozens of dams, glinting in the sunlight. To the north lies Stellenbosch, to the south, a cluster of small towns: Somerset West in the foreground and Gordon's Bay and Strand on the shores of False Bay.

From here walk back along the ridge and look out for the markers at the far end. There are several cairns along the ridge which are easier to see on the way back than on the way up. The descent to the contour path is very steep and sometimes worn; go down slowly. Take particular care on the last section of the descent from the high saddle above Stellenboschkloof: the path is covered in loose stones. The journey from the summit of the Dome to the Porcupine saddle takes about 1h (**4h45min**). From here the route back is down Porcupine Buttress, the way you came up. This too is very steep in places and requires more care than on the ascent. However, it should take no more than 1h50min to reach the bottom (**6h35min**). Or, if you have the time and energy, you can return over the top of the Western Peak, following the path described in Walk 19, or divert along any of the colour-coded contour paths further down the mountainside. The restaurant in the reserve can do wonders for the morale after a tiring walk.

21 PERDEKOP

Distance/time: 17km/10.5mi; 6h15min

Grade: strenuous — more on account of its length than the steepness of the terrain. There is a good path to within a few hundred metres of the summit, at which point a number of strategically-placed cairns guide the way to the top. Climb 1000m/3300ft.

Equipment: walking boots, sunhat, jersey, waterproofs, picnic (and extra high-calorie rations), water, whistle, compass, area map (for the views); long-sleeved shirt and suncream in sunny weather. There are streams 2km from the start of the walk and near the summit, but nowhere else.

How to get there and return: 🚗 Follow Car tour 5 via Stellenbosch and the Helshoogtepas to the top of Franschhoekpas (see page 28). Here a very rough gravel track cuts back sharply to the left: drive along it for about 0.5km, then park by a gate (normally closed, preventing further progress up the track).

Permits: *All versions of this walk require permits,* which should be obtained in advance either from the Municipal Offices or the Information Centre in Franschhoek (nominal cost). The Municipal Offices (tel: 876 2505; closed Sat/Sun) are on the left-hand side of the main road about halfway through the town, behind green lawns; the Information Centre (tel: 876 3603; late opening Sat/Sun) is on the right, just beyond a bridge over a stream, as the road bends right after entering Franschhoek.

Alternative walks: Two alternatives are described here, both featuring outstanding scenery. In fact, the area is so beautiful that it might pay to spend a night or two at one of the area's many guest houses. There is a lot more to do besides walking for one thing, and for another the logistics will be much simpler.

1 Olifantshoek. 9km/5.6mi; 3h15m. Moderate. Climb 500m/1640ft. Equipment and access as main walk. Follow the main walk to the cairn near the head of the valley (1h20min). Then keep straight ahead (instead of turning right). Walk for another 350m/yds, to a look-out point high above a huge gorge with high mountains rising on the far side. This is Olifantshoek (Elephant's Corner), and the view is no less breathtaking than the one you get from the main walk. Amongst the peaks you can see from here are the Pinnacle and the Peaklet, smaller free-standing pillars that jut out from the massif behind them. Return by the same route.

2 Dutoitskop. 8km/5mi; 3h30min. Strenuous. Climb 670m/2200ft. Equipment and access as main walk, but *take plenty of water* — there is none en route. Take an area map, too: the view from the top is enormous. Follow the main walk to the path marked 'Dutoitskop' (30min) and fork left. From here the path is reasonably clear, choosing a relatively painless way to the reach the summit. Be sure to keep left at a fork about three-quarters of the way up. And note that when the path scrambles over outcrops of rock (which happens fairly frequently), it almost always emerges on the upper side of the outcrop. Return the same way.

This walk is in high mountainous territory to the north-east of Franschhoek, 90km to the northeast of Cape Town, in the heart of the Boland. Starting on the top of the Franschhoekpas some 750m/2460ft above sea level and rising to the summit of Perdekop (Horse's Head), 1575m/5166ft above sea level, it is a lonely walk in isolated and beautiful country, exposed to the whims of sun, wind and rain. So choose your day carefully: it is an area of extremes.

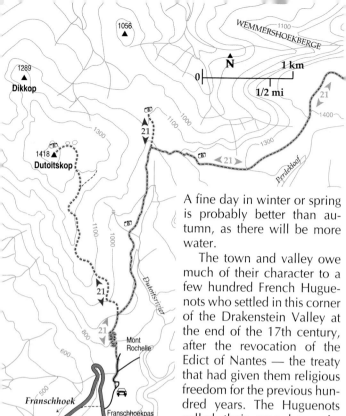

A fine day in winter or spring is probably better than autumn, as there will be more water.

The town and valley owe much of their character to a few hundred French Huguenots who settled in this corner of the Drakenstein Valley at the end of the 17th century, after the revocation of the Edict of Nantes — the treaty that had given them religious freedom for the previous hundred years. The Huguenots called their new home Le Quartier Français — before the Dutch insisted it be changed to its present name. Be that as it may, France's loss has turned out to be the Cape's gain. The French influence is everywhere, from the names of the farms and the people, to the grapes and the country cooking. The combination of Swiss scenery, Cape hospitality and French cuisine is irresistible.

Having arrived at the starting point by the gate, **begin the walk** by going to the left of the gate and taking the path in front of you, short cutting a bend in the track. The track soon curves back again and you have no option but to follow it. You pass another track off to the right and then fork obliquely to the left on an uphill path (just before the track ends in a small copse, about 0.5km/0.3mi from the gate). The path zigzags slowly up the hillside ahead, before curving to the right and reaching a brow (**30min**). *(Alternative walk 2 follows the path to the left here, signposted 'Dutoitskop'.)* Behind you, to the south, the wide Theewaterskloofdam, Cape Town's chief source of water, spreads out in the distance, where the Dutoitsrivier joins

the Riviersonderende — the river without end. Carry on along the main path as it dips down and traverses the side of a long valley, rising to a distant saddle. A strong stream flows at the foot of the valley on your right (Dutoitsrivier). The path soon levels out and crosses a stream by a wooden bridge, about 2km/1.2mi from the gate. This is one of only two waterholes on the route. If you look up to the left there is a waterfall higher up, spilling over a series of rock faces — a fine spectacle after rain.

The path rises after crossing the stream, then dips again towards the river, before turning uphill once more towards the distant saddle. Eventually it reaches a large cairn just before the saddle, where another path goes off to the right (**1h20min**). *(Alternative walk 1 goes straight ahead at this cairn.)* Take the path to the right; it soon climbs out of the valley, clambering amongst a succession of small rocky outcrops. Any one of these outcrops can be used as a look-out point to the north, where the scenery changes suddenly in a most spectacular fashion. You are now climbing along the southern border of a huge ravine: Olifantshoek (Elephant's Corner). This vast gorge carries water from the Olifantsrivier and its many tributaries to a beautiful reservoir further downstream to the left: Wemmershoekdam.

The gorge has four fingers etched deeply into the rock, many hundreds of metres deep. You are standing just next to the little finger, near its base, gazing across at the Wemmershoekberge on the far side, its rocky chain of summits and saddles rising 1400m/4600ft above the silent river far below — an awe-inspiring sight. From the topmost of the rocks, the path begins to level out and continues its eastern journey in a more leisurely way. After a while it rises again to the left, still on well-trodden sand and rock, sometimes running with water in winter and spring, but dry as a bone in summer. At the top of the long rise there are a number of curiously shaped rocks, cleaned white by wind and rain (**2h30min**). The horizons are very wide: nearly everything you look at seems to be below your feet. Table Mountain can be seen on the southwestern horizon, with Devil's Peak and Lion's Head to the right. Further east, on the southern horizon, are the high mountains overlooking False Bay: Somerset Sneeukop, the Triplets, Haelkop — and Simonsberg's six peaks to the right of Table Mountain, at the summit of Helshoogtepas.

About 30 minutes later you arrive at a fork. The left-hand path goes on forever into higher mountains still, where it

View over the Wemmershoekdam from the vantage point overlooking the Olifantshoek. Klein Drakenstein is just behind the dam, while the peak on the left is Dikkop (Fathead).

vanishes without trace in a steep and craggy wilderness — a different world, where it is easy to get lost, and beyond the scope of this book. So take the right-hand path; it begins to lose altitude almost at once — slowly at first, then more rapidly (after turning to the right at a cairn about 200 paces from the fork). After descending some 30m/100ft, the path comes to a marsh of green feathery reeds, with a stream at its centre, flowing swiftly down to the right. This is the second waterhole, and it's a real beauty — the water soft and cold. This marsh is close to one of the sources of the Dutoitsrivier at the top of Perdekloof, the longest of all the streams running into the river. Look at the lower reaches of the stream on the return journey, before you reach the wooden bridge again. There are some lovely waterfalls on that side of the river too, higher up than the one above the bridge. Those streams seem to flow all the year round.

Beyond the marsh, the path swings left and starts its steady ascent to the summit of Perdekop, now very close. The path peters out after a few hundred metres/yards, but cairns are placed at intervals all the way to the top. For once there are no false horizons; the summit appears suddenly, decorated by the cairn shown opposite — a stone beacon that would not disgrace Westminster Abbey (**3h30min**). This carefully-constructed monument stands some 1575m/5166ft above sea level, a vantage point sculptured like a pulpit, deep into the mountains. Nothing impedes the view from here. The ground falls away all around you, gently to begin with, and then more steeply, to a kaleidoscope of deep gorges which come together at

Cairn on Perdekop

a lonely reservoir — Stettyns-kloofdam. Range after range of mountains march towards the distant horizons: Klein Draken-stein to the west, the Wemmers-hoekberge (on which Perdekop stands) to the south and north-west, the Dutoitsberge to the north, the Stettynsberge to the east, and the Boland ranges to the southwest. But the land-scape is so vast that its details are all but lost: nameless gorges separating lonely peaks, and anonymous rocks overlooking shadowy streams. Few travellers have passed this way, with tales of dramatic encounters to illustrate and enliven the maps.

The journey back from this wilderness retraces the outward path, which seems longer than on the way out, particularly by the banks of the Dutoitsrivier. However, there are compensations, including the afternoon shadows that paint the lakes and peaks in a subtler light, revealing silhouettes that were lost in the blandness of the morning sun. And there is still plenty of wild life in these mountains, although it is becoming increasingly shy. Baboons, rhe-buck and dassies are relatively common — as well as *duiker* and hare. The ubiquitous lizard is no stranger to this terrain either — darting out of your moving shadow or nodding in the sun. All have much keener hearing than sight, incidentally, so that silence is more likely to yield results than conversation.

A further point to note is that the municipality is plan-ning to open up more paths in this area — when it can muster the necessary resources. As a result, the paths described here may eventually connect with others, to form a network of circular routes instead of the present linear walk. In the meantime, please stick to the existing paths. The walk back to the gate should take about 2h45min — allowing for the many ups and downs that went unnoticed on the outward journey! This brings your total walking time to **6h15min**.

22 SOMERSET-SNEEUKOP FROM THE JONKERSHOEK NATURE RESERVE

See also photograph page 130-131

Distance/time: 21km/13mi; 8h

Grade: very strenuous, both up and down. You must be sure-footed. Climb 1450m/4755ft. Arrive early; *the walking time given does not allow for stops* (see 'How to get there').

Equipment: walking boots, sunhat, jersey, waterproof, picnic, water (although there is no shortage of water en route). *It is not a good idea to undertake this walk in summer,* when the reserve is normally far too hot and dry, so suncream and long-sleeved shirts are not necessary.

How to get there: 🚗 Follow Car tour 5 to Stellenbosch and start driving up Helshoogtepas beyond the traffic lights outside the town (see page 26). But only a few hundred metres further on, take the next road to the right. Turn left when it arrives at a T-junction. Follow this road until it ends at the Jonkershoek Gate. *Note that the gates to the reserve open at 7.30am and close at 5pm.* Permits are obtained at the gate for a small fee. Your parking place is 3km beyond the gate: continue by car along a jeep track, keeping right at a fork. Cross a wooden bridge over the Eersterivier — the 'Swartbrug' (Black Bridge). Then, after veering left, pass a large dam on the left. Shortly afterwards, the track winds its bumpy way to a rudimentary car park in a small clearing on the left.

Alternative walk: Sosyskloof. 10km/6.2mi; 3h20min. Easy. Access, equipment as main walk. Climb 320m/1050ft. Park at the reserve gate, and follow the notes for motorists above to *walk* to the car park used for the main walk. From here follow the main walk to the contour path at the scree (the 45min-point in the main walk; 1h45min in this version). Then turn right and continue along the contour path in a wide arc, until it passes under a waterfall in the Sosyskloof and curves round to an observation hut. Beyond the hut, follow the zigzag path downhill, and turn left a few zigzags down. This path traverses diagonally downhill and meets a jeep track, which you follow to the left for about 30 paces. From there the path descends to a second jeep track, which leads left, back to the gate.

Jonkershoek is the name given to the whole valley, not just the nature reserve where this walk takes place. The countryside weaves its magic long before the gates are reached: a secret refuge for the laying of urban ghosts — the ghosts that haunt every countryman who makes a living in town. The atmosphere pervading this beautiful valley is both powerful and serene, the texture of its scent and silence driving out all else from the brain. This is the heart of the Cape and its rural culture: a land of plenty.

Jonkershoek (Jonker's Corner) is named after a Dutchman who started farming in the area some 300 years ago: one Jan Andriesson de Jonker. He acquired the land in 1683, when the Cape of Good Hope was administered by the Dutch East India Company. On his death in 1698, the farm was granted to a slave called Jan van Ceylon. He had been freed by the then governor of the Cape, Simon van der Stel, whose enlightened policy was perhaps inspired by his own mixed blood.

The Hottentots-Holland mountains, with Somerset-Sneeukop to the left of the tree (view from the ascent in Walks 19 and 20)

As you drive (main walk) or walk (Alternative walk) to the car park 3km beyond the gate, the scenery is dominated by high mountains: great rocky fortresses rearing upwards to the left, and a steeply-sloping ridge to the right. The fortresses start with the Twin Peaks, towering some 1200m/4000ft above the track and 1500m/5000ft above the sea. Further along are the Ridge Peaks, just as high and even craggier than the Twins. Behind your left shoulder lie the Square Tower and the rest of the Jonkershoekberge, culminating in Bothma's Peak, rising abruptly above Stellenbosch. To the right, standing almost directly opposite the car park, the stately Haelkop (1384m/4540ft high) marks the topmost point of the Stellenboschberge.

Start the walk at a signpost on the far side of the track: it points towards a stony path leading to Swartboskloof (Black Bush Ravine), and this is the route to follow. The mountains slope upwards more gently here, so that one has time to adjust one's mind and legs to the huge horizons in relative comfort. The path is a good one, going against the grain of one of a number of hiking trails in these mountains that take from two to three days to complete. This particular section forms the second day of a two-day trail that on the first day leads to an overnight hut called Landdroskop (Sheriff's Head), 17.6km to the south of the Jonkershoek Gate. The second day's walk includes the descent of Swartboskloof, a formidable hurdle with a heavy pack and no mean task with a light one either. But first we have to climb it — and a great deal more besides, for by the end of the afternoon we will have climbed and descended some 1450m, much of it on uneven terrain.

To begin with the way is easy — more or less level. After about 600m/0.4mi, the path forks left and crosses a tumble-

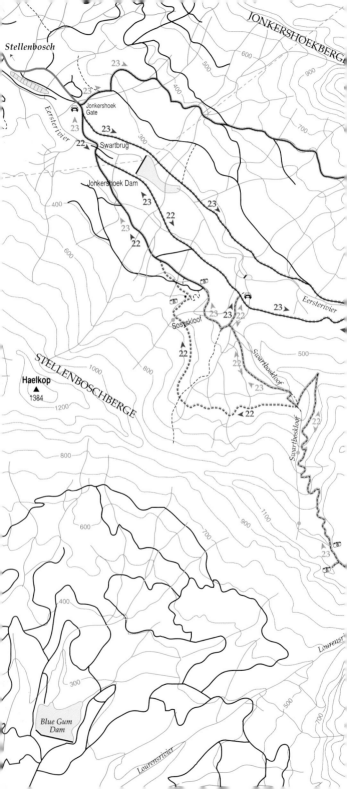

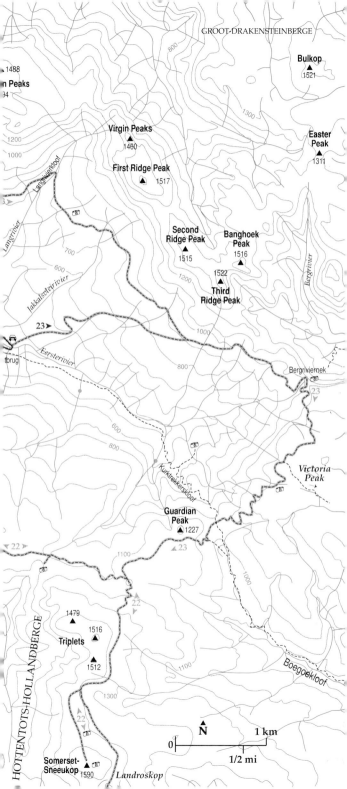

down wooden bridge over one of the countless mountain streams that pour into the Eersterivier, all carrying clean sparkling water. The water is sometimes as pure as crystal and sometimes tinted with a hue as light as a fine brandy — its colour caused by the presence of humic acid leached from the soil. The path begins to rise beyond the bridge, as it wanders southeast alongside a bigger and noisier stream approaching the river after its rumbustious journey down Swartboskloof. The stream runs some distance below the path for the next kilometre or so, flowing between the path and a slowly-rising ridge to the east: Bobbejaansrand (Baboons Ridge). This section of the walk alternates between long stretches of stony ground and shorter interludes of soft sand. The *fynbos* is thick and tall, often colourful and sometimes heavily scented — particularly in early spring.

The path rises more steeply after a while, twisting backwards and forwards before crossing a broad scree. The path then rejoins the scree, where a contour path comes in obliquely from the right (**45min**). *(The Alternative walk turns right at this point.)* The route now follows the contour path in a southeasterly direction for a short distance, before bending abruptly to the left and stumbling over the Swartboskloof stream. Shortly afterwards it doubles back right and starts up the *kloof* in earnest.

The path winds its steady way up the left-hand side of the ravine until it closes with the stream again, just above the first of two waterfalls. It is full of fury in the rain, spray rising in a northwest wind, but gentler after the wind has dropped. After climbing through a dark wood, where a tributary flows in from the left, the *kloof* widens, becoming open and boulder-strewn. Cairns are placed at strategic intervals, as the path steepens and begins a series of wide zigzags towards the upper reaches of the ravine. As the path climbs out of the *kloof* to the left, some 850m/2800ft above the road, it crosses yet another stream, one of many that pour into the ravine from all angles. This one is wide and strong and carries the sweetest drinking water imaginable. Now your route follows a straight rise of rocks, before a clear path over undulating terrain finally takes you to the top of the ravine (**2h15min**).

The texture of the *fynbos* changes at this point, no longer bristling with heather and bush, but interspersed with more and more *Restionaceae* — tall reeds or rushes with strong stems and golden crowns. As the path moves further south, the reeds form colourful meadows, enriched by the sunlight. Note that the path is close to the top of the Hottentots-

Holland escarpment on this section — a feature which will be explored on the way back. Some distance from the top of the ravine, the path swings to the left (east) and begins to lose altitude again, descending gradually and then more steeply into a high valley some 75m/250ft below the brow. Then, as the path rises from the valley again, the terrain becomes rockier and more difficult to penetrate, as prickly *fynbos* once more crowds the stumbling path — until another fast-flowing stream is reached (**3h**).

Very soon afterwards the path rises to an oblique junction, where a path cutting back left leads to the head of the Jonkershoek Valley. The path to Somerset-Sneeukop goes straight on here, its surface hard particles of white crystallised rock. There used to be a sort of Druid's circle set in a landscape littered with rock just above this point, where the path moves to the right. But the left-hand arc of the circle has fallen into disuse and is now overgrown: you don't see it until you're on top of it. The rocks are still there, as well as the path leading to it, which clambers up a rocky outcrop in steep zigzags.

Over the next 2km/1.2mi the path gradually climbs across the scree-scarred slopes of a trio of peaks called the Triplets, rising steeply to the right. A deep valley lies to the left, its far wall lined with exposed rock faces — perfect

This spectacular waterfall in Sosys-kloof is one of the high points of the Alternative walk. It flows over the path like a curtain of crystal, the rock behind it lavishly clothed in bright green reeds and moss. The word 'kloof', incidentally, which is used by Afrikaners and English speakers alike, is not pronounced as in 'roof' but as 'kluerf' — the 'er' very briefly — a rough and ready noun that describes these rugged ravines with an onomatopoeic aptness.

View of the Ridge Peaks from the high valley above Jonkershoek, just before the path rises to the Druid's circle. Guardian Peak rises to the right.

examples of geological folding. As the valley comes to a head, so does the path. Having passed the Triplets, it reaches a stream idling through marshy ground at the head of the valley. The path bends to the left here and makes for Landdroskop, some 6km/3.7mi away. But this is where travellers to Somerset-Sneeukop strike off right and head towards a saddle lying between Somerset and the third Triplet — at a point where the escarpment bends in unison with the path. A brief battle with a tall tangle of dark green reeds growing in sodden black soil brings you to the saddle. The saddle, for the record, lies at about 1450m/ 4750ft and gives way to an expansive array of scenery across False Bay — and more especially to some staggering country at your feet. Huge and steep ravines fall away to left, right and centre between craggy outriders to the main escarpment. Helderberg is there on your right, the Dome's summit over 300m/1000ft below this saddle.

The ascent to the top (140m/460ft) isn't technically difficult. There is no path: just follow the lie of the land to the left and find your own way up (keeping to the right of a wide thicket of protea near the beginning). There are a few thick layers of rock to climb and a few false horizons to overcome, but the summit is soon reached (**4h30min**). The survey beacon stands 1590m/5217ft above sea level, the highest point for many a mile. All around lie endless seascapes, landscapes and sky. To the south the Hottentots-Holland range runs down to the northeastern shores of False Bay, while beyond it another range of mountains called Kogelberge takes over the baton and runs along the eastern shore until the bay opens out into the ocean. The view to the west takes in the whole of the bay and the entire length of the peninsula, including the familiar profiles of Lion's Head, Devil's Peak, Table Mountain and Constantiaberg. Elsewhere the scenery comprises mountains — one range after another rolling into the distance. Somerset-Sneeukop actually stands at a point very close to where the five ridges in this network of mountains fan out in a semicircle to the east. The Hottentots-Holland and Stellenbosch ridges form the diameter or base-line from which the Franschhoek, Groot-Drakenstein and Jonkershoek ridges spread out from east to northwest in a variable radius, 20 to 30 kilometres long. But these mountains, impressive as they are, form only part of the landscape: beyond them are bigger mountains still, including the magnificent Wemmershoekberge and Dutoitsberge which rise higher and higher into the eastern and northern skies.

There is plenty of room on Somerset-Sneeukop's summit, including what looks like a brace of shepherd's pens. On a cold day their stone walls, recessed into natural hollows big enough to shelter several dozen sheep, provide good shelter for a picnic lunch. Remember to *drink* as well as eat: cramp comes easily on these high mountains.

The return journey is more interesting than one would expect, considering that it retraces the outward journey exactly, but things always look different from the opposite angle. To begin with, make sure you keep far enough to the left to get back to the rocky saddle: further right the terrain is much bushier. Having regained the path, the next thing to look out for is the way down the steep descent to the Druid's circle: it is not easy to find at first, as it's badly signposted. After the path clears the Triplets again, watch for a series of stone cairns built with the same material as the underlying brown rock; they are on the right.

Just before the path climbs up again from the high valley described on the way out, there is another path going off left towards a low hilltop about fifty paces from the main trail (**5h45min**). From there the ground falls away between high cliffs into a very steep ravine, through which the Lourensrivier flows before edging past Somerset West into False Bay. The ravine is called Diepgat (Deep Gap or Hole), and the view from the hilltop is worth the effort: the cliffs frame a picture of the rolling uplands and the shoreline, with the bay and peninsula in the distant background. About 1km/0.6mi further on, another path goes to the escarpment. Again a climb is involved, but the view is even better than the previous one. This time the escarpment drops straight down from where you're standing, providing a much clearer view of the bay and peninsula — and the quilted countryside at your feet. Nearby, the Helderberg Dome partly hides the western horizon.

A few minutes later you reach the top of Swartboskloof (**6h30min**). Like most mountain scenery, its mood depends upon the light but, given the season and the time of day, the sun could well be casting a slanting light across the pinnacles and buttresses of the Ridge Peaks, picking them out in sharp detail against the mass of rock behind them. By contrast, the nearer of the Twins, to the left of the Ridge Peaks, rises in a series of almost sheer faces, towering over the remainder of the ridge beyond it. Far below, the valley slopes down to the left, the course of the Eersterivier at its centre hidden by trees and bushes, until the river runs into the silvery dam about a kilometre from the gate. The wide and deep ravine below is dotted with grey and lichen-covered rock, with a labyrinth of streams plunging down the mountainside between boulders, bush and wind-swept trees. Glimpses of Stellenbosch and a multi-steepled mountain beyond the Jonkershoekberge can be seen too: Simonsberg (photograph pages 28-29) — named after one of the early Huguenots, Paul Simon. From a certain angle it looks like Napoleon lying on his back, his hat on his head and his hands folded on his tummy. But that view is not the one you see from the top of this *kloof:* from here only three of its six peaks are visible, the mountain looking more like a prehistoric reptile than a French emperor.

It goes without saying that the descent isn't easy, the surface of the path unremitting rock and stone. However, the ravine has its compensations, for it is one of the most beautiful in the region, renowned for the richness of its flora and host to thousands of different species of plant. (A battalion of botanists has been absorbed in its exploration for years.) There is the little wood where the two streams come together, too — a refreshing spot to take a break, before pressing on to the track at the bottom (**8h**).

The drive out continues along the elliptical anti-clockwise track for about 2km, before it crosses the Eersterivier for the second time — over the sturdy Witbrug. From there the track turns sharply to the left, back to the gate.

The Ridge Peaks from Sosyskloof (Alternative walk)

23 THE JONKERSHOEK PANORAMA ROUTE

See map pages 122-123; see also photographs pages 126 and 128

Distance/time: 25km/15.5mi; 8h35min

Grade: very strenuous. This is one of the classic walks of the region — and one of the longest, too, with a great deal of climbing (steady rather than abrupt) and an equal amount of descending — not as steady, most of it occurring all at once towards the end of the hike. *Note that the overall time will be well over 9h: start early!* (The gates open at 7.30am and close at 5pm). Climb 1250m/4100ft.

Equipment: walking boots, sunhat, jersey, waterproofs, compass, first-aid kit, plenty of high-energy food and water; long trousers and gloves in cold weather. There is no shortage of water in the streams en route; drink frequently: most forms of liquid are great energy providers, and water particularly reduces the chances of cramp. *It is not a good idea to undertake this walk in summer,* when the reserve is normally far too hot and dry, so suncream and long-sleeved shirts are not necessary.

How to get there and return: as Walk 22, page 120, *but park as for the Alternative walk.*

Short walk: Jonkershoek Valley. 10km/6.2mi; 2h30min. Easy. Equipment: stout walking shoes. Access as Walk 22, page 120, *but park as for the Alternative walk.* This walk follows a gently undulating jeep track all the way. Walk through the gate and follow the main jeep track, keeping left at the first fork and then following the elliptical route through the valley in a clockwise direction back to the gate. Autumn or spring are the best times, when there is plenty of colour in both the trees and the *fynbos.*

Alternative walk: Shorter panorama route. 18km/11.2mi; 6h35min. Grade and equipment as main walk. Climb 1200m/3940ft. Access as Walk 22 (page 120), *but follow the jeep track all the way to its end* and park on the right, beyond the bridge over the Eersterivier (the Witbrug). Walk down the track, with the river on your left, then take a path off right, signposted 'Panorama Roete' (about 200m/yds from the car). This path climbs to the contour path described in the main walk, which you will reach after about 1h15min; a large cairn marks the junction. From here pick up the main walk at the 2h45min-point, making suitable time adjustments. Leave the main walk at the 7h35min-point: walk on to the jeep track and turn right along it, back to your car.

T his walk circumnavigates the whole Jonkershoek Valley by a route shaped like a long horseshoe: its closed arch lies high above the Witbrug, and its two sides come together again at the Jonkershoek Gate. At its highest point, the path reaches an altitude of over 1300m/4265ft, at its lowest, near the Swartbrug, 240m/787ft. For most of the 25km journey the track winds through open country, over-looking the long valley below, its sloping flanks bejewelled with waterfalls, streams and trees. Occasionally the path is hidden by high *fynbos* or dense woodland, while at one stage — as it joins the route to Somerset-Sneeukop — it leaves the valley altogether and becomes lost in lonely mountain landscapes. Given the right day — cold and fine — it is the most enchanting and exhilarating of walks, the perfect precursor to a hot bath and a gourmandiser's dinner.

The Ridge Peaks from near the Jonkershoek Gate

But before the enjoyment starts, there is the customary long drive in the darkness of early morning and the growing light of dawn, through low-lying mists and over hills that give way to black mountains sharply silhouetted against an orange strip of sky. These are the things that soothe the early riser, the fumbler in the dark, the eater of a silent breakfast, the traveller dumbly cocooned in a warm, murmuring motor car…

There are two versions of this hike. The longer one has been chosen because its easy rhythm suits a long stride. The shorter one (the Alternative walk) is good too, but involves another jolting ride on the gravel road and an early battle with the force of gravity.

The walk starts just inside the reserve gate: take the path to the left, soon following a jeep track that continues left past the forestry settlement and then bends right into the depths of the reserve. The track rises steadily for 0.5km/ 0.3mi or so, until it reaches another one going off left again at a right-angled junction. Turn left and follow the new track as it bends to the right shortly afterwards and curls uphill through pine plantations and swathes of indigenous trees and *fynbos*. Turn right at a T-junction (**40min**) and follow the track through thick pine woods as it traverses the mountainside for some distance. Then, just as it appears you might spend all day on level ground, meandering in and out of deep gullies, you branch off left on another track (**55min**) and begin climbing steadily through the trees.

Keep to this track (ignoring another coming in from the left) until the gradient slackens as the track leaves the treeline and arrives at a fork, where you go left (**1h15min**). This section climbs relentlessly for some time, before bending to the right and levelling off at last. After contouring steadily for some distance, the track bends left and comes to an end, about 5km/3mi from the gate. A narrow and overgrown path takes over from here, hugging a rising rock face to the left and a steeply-banked and densely-wooded

path reaches the Langrivier (Long River) and crosses it over a jumble of large and slippery boulders — 700m/2300ft above sea level and 450m/1475ft above the gate (**1h45min**). This crossing is a good place to stop and take in some refreshments. The water is fast-flowing and delicious. On top of that, the ravine has a dark beauty which is hard to match — completely shaded from sun, wind and rain by the leaf canopy of closely growing evergreens. The *kloof* rises steeply to the left, climbing to a high saddle between the Twins and the Virgin Peaks.

The path now moves steadily upwards along the far bank of the *kloof* and begins a very long traverse across the mountainside below the rocky cliffs supporting the Ridge Peaks. This section is often overgrown with protea and other scratchy bushes. However, it has its compensations: the scenery across the valley to the right, towards the Stellenboschberge, and up to the Ridge Peaks on the left, is very fine indeed. At one point, the jagged saddle overlooking Langrivierkloof becomes clear, silhouetted against the sky behind you.

Some 3km beyond the Langrivierkloof, the path is joined by another path rising obliquely from the valley below (the Boland Hiking Trail; **2h45min**). The junction is marked by a large cairn — the second one since leaving the *kloof*. (*This is where the Alternative walk joins the main route.*)

Note that both this path and the previous one, about halfway along, provide emergency exits in bad weather.

From the cairn the path continues to traverse in a south-easterly direction, leaving the valley floor well behind. The sloping mountainside consists of a series of deep and wide folds, the original rock debris covered in thick *fynbos* and cut deeply by the incessant passage of water. Ahead, the landscape is dominated by the high ridge of mountains forming the closed arch of the horseshoe, with a steep gully to the right of it leading up to a mountain called Guardian Peak. At the top of the gully lies a distinctive rock shaped like a ship's rudder, a landmark that is visible for most of the morning's journey… but more of that later.

After swinging through a very deep gully and another smaller one, the path begins to travel through a thicket of yellow daisies — in flower from late September to early November. The thicket is tall, hiding the hiker completely. Then the path begins to climb again, and wide tracts of the mountainside open out — ablaze with yellow, or clothed in a darker green — depending on the season. As the path rises further, it bends left and makes for a high saddle sitting between two buttresses: the Ridge Peaks have at last been circumnavigated, some 11km/6.8mi from the gate (**3h 30min**). *Please note that **it is dangerous to press on from here in bad weather:** retrace your steps back to the previous cairn and take the path down left into the valley, where you can follow the jeep track back to the gate.*

The sheer grandeur of the scene that greets the eye from this saddle (called Bergriviernek because of its proximity to the Bergrivier's source) baffles description. It is literally breathtaking. The source of the river, and several of its early tributaries, lies high up on the left, between the Third Ridge Peak and Banghoek Peak behind it. The water from these streams falls down a labyrinth of precipitous ravines scoured from fantastic granite buttresses and pinnacles — heights that soar upwards to the sharp blue sky above and plunge down to the lonely valley below. This long valley runs down to the east (towards Franschhoek) and is called Assegaaiboskloof (Assegaai-Bush Ravine). This tree grows in the deep *kloofs* of Zululand too, where the wood was used to make stabbing spears in days gone by. To the right of Bergriviernek, opposite Banghoek Peak, dark cliffs rise, huge and precipitous, outriders of higher mountains beyond — including the 1589m/5214ft-high Victoria Peak. Down the valley, distant mountains give way to the Klein-Drakensteinberge (Little Dragon Mountains) and the high and lonely Wemmershoekberge beyond. In the opposite direction, across the Jonkershoek Valley to the south, are the Triplets, towering over Guardian Peak.

Bergriviernek stands at 1150m/3772ft above sea level, so that the path has already risen 900m/2950ft from the gate, a goodly portion of the total ascent. But before the gradient levels out, there is a steep climb to the right of the saddle on a path that executes a careful and stony zigzag, before moving further over to the right, traversing along a route overlooking the earlier path. Eventually the path turns left alongside a beautiful ravine, carrying one of the main tributaries of the Eersterivier. The path soon crosses the stream and then follows it towards its source further to the southeast, before switching to the right once more and starting its traverse across the head of the valley, still slowly gaining altitude. The *fynbos* changes character at this point, a liberal mix of reeds competing with clumps of sturdy heather, the rutted path sometimes running with water. Occasionally, the insectivorous plant, *Drosera,* displays its sticky auburn flowers in a web of small hairy leaves, waiting to devour an unsuspecting ant or beetle. This area is also frequented by game: klipspringer and grey rhebuck in particular. The former (its name means 'rock jumper' in English) is a small antelope with short straight horns and a loud voice, frequently used by the sentinel to warn its companions of approaching danger. The rhebuck looks similar from a distance, but is bigger, with long ears.

As the path rises and falls at an altitude of 1200m/3940ft and more, it circumnavigates the fingers of one beautiful ravine after another, sometimes revealing distant horizons well beyond the boundaries of the reserve, way out to sea and down the peninsula. There is a path going off at one point, about 1km/0.6mi from the neck, making towards the top of the rise on the left: it leads to Victoria Peak. Soon after this junction, your path swings left and starts a gradual downhill perambulation round another ravine before rising and falling again and coming to a rocky platform just at the head of the valley — some 13km/8mi from the gate. This vantage point makes an excellent lunch stop.

The path descends fairly steeply afterwards, twisting down in a series of tight turns to the neck below Guardian Peak (**4h30min**). The peak's summit, 1227m/4024ft high, gradually disappears behind a nearer shoulder, as the path drops down to the rock that looks like a ship's rudder… but the name of the gorge below it is Kurktrekkerskloof (Cork-screw Ravine). Perhaps the rock looked like the head of a corkscrew to the map-maker. Be that as it may, the ravine makes a good escape route in an emergency, though the path is very loose and stony. It leads straight down to the valley and then alongside the river for about 3km/2mi, before meeting the jeep track near the Witbrug.

Opposite the path down Kurktrekkerskloof, another path goes off to the southeast, towards Boegoekloof. It is part of the Boland Hiking Trail network and closed from April to October because of the risk of flooding. The panorama path now leaves the saddle, climbing across the southeastern flank of Guardian Peak. After a zigzag ascent some 130m/425ft high, the path continues round Guardian Peak to the right and then breaks off southwards. From there it heads towards the Triplets, after about 2km/1.2mi arriving at a junction of paths near an overgrown Druid's circle (**5h15min**; see Walk 22 and photograph page 126).

From here the route is the same as Walk 22: pick up those notes from just after the 5h45min-point (page 127). You traverse the high valley and descend Swartboskloof to the wooden bridge just before the path reaches the jeep track (**7h35min**). From this point, however, we take a different route to the gate: turn left after crossing the bridge and follow a path that runs parallel with the track for about 1km/0.6mi. *(But for the Alternative walk, carry on to the track.)* After crossing a major stream, the path climbs again and pushes through thick undergrowth, before meeting a jeep track at a hairpin bend. High above to the left is a fire-watcher's hut. This bend offers a fine panorama, a last opportunity to survey the scene, before following the track down through pine forests — until it joins the main track near the Swartbrug and returns to the gate (**8h35min**).

Klipspringer country — soon after the path winds past Guardian Peak

Index

Geographical names comprise the only entries in this index; for non-geographical subjects, see Contents, page 3. A page number in *italic type* indicates a map; **bold type** refers to a photograph. Both of these may be in addition to a text reference on the same page. 'TM' refers to the large-scale (1:13,000) walking map on the reverse of the touring map.

135

Glossary of Afrikaans or Dutch names

baai bay

berg — mountain

blinkwater — glittering water

bobbejaan — baboon

boer — farmer

bos/bosch — bush

bosboustasie — forestry station

brug — bridge

buffel — buffalo

dassie — rock rabbit

die — the

dorp — town

duivel — devil

eerste — first

eiland — island

ein — one

els — alder

fontein — spring

Fransch — French

fynbos — narrow-leafed bush

gat — hole

geel — yellow

groen — green

groot — large

grot — cave

hael — hail

heuvel — hill

hoek — corner

hoer — high

hout — wood or timber

kalk — lime

kasteel — castle

klein — little

klip — rock or stone

kloof — ravine or gorge

kop — head or hill

lang — long

leeu — lion

myn — mine

nek — neck

noord — north

olifant — elephant

pad — path

pas — pass

piek — peak

plek — place

poort — gate

punt — point

rand — ridge

rivier — river

ronde — round

rooi — red

rot — rock

sirkel — circle

skiereiland — peninsula

slang — snake

smitswinkel — blacksmith

sneeu — snow

sosys — sausage

springer — jumper

stad — city

stein/steen — stone

sterk — steep

strand — beach

swart — black

tafel — table

tuin — garden

tweede — second

uitkyk — lookout

vallei — valley

van — of

vis — fish

vlakte — plain

voorbrand — firebreak

wit — white

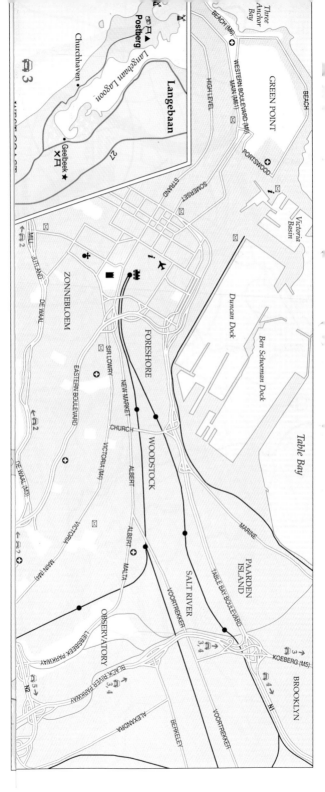